The Chicken Ranch

The True Story of the
Best Little Whorehouse in Texas

Jan Hutson

Authors Choice Press
San Jose New York Lincoln Shanghai

The Chicken Ranch

The Chicken Ranch
The True Story of the Best Little Whorehouse in Texas

Authors Choice Press
an imprint of iUniverse.com, Inc.

For information address:
iUniverse.com, Inc.
620 North 48th Street
Suite 201
Lincoln, NE 68504-3467
www.iuniverse.com

Originally published by A. S. Barnes & Company

ISBN: 0-595-12848-3

Printed in the United States of America

From the lower depths of the dormitory a voice could be heard shouting "Chicken Farm" over and over again, the weekly call for the carload driving to the country whorehouse in La Grange.

–Willie Morris,
North toward Home

Contents

Acknowledgments

Writing a book is a very private experience and this was no exception, but it could not have been done without help and support from my family. I thank them all . . . my husband Jean for his enthusiasm in humoring my eccentricities, and my children, Jon, Kim, and Robin, for their patience and their pride. I hope they will all be willing to furnish more of the same for my future efforts.

Introduction

Although the Texas Rangers, some Hardshell Baptists, and a few jealous wives tried, it was solely through the efforts of one small, toupeed, shoulder-padded TV reporter that the infamous Chicken Ranch was forced out of business. The sign on the gate reading CLOSED BY ORDER OF MARVIN ZINDLER also wrote finis to America's oldest continuously operating whorehouse.

If the Texas Archives have been negligent in recording any date of establishment or any other matter pertaining to one of the State's most famous and entertaining business enterprises, the Texas Historical Society and the Texas Heritage Commission have been remiss in their duties as well. A historical medallion on the front porch would seem in order, or at the very least, a historic marker. Fortunately, the data not available from official records has been recorded in the minds of several generations of talkative Texans, satisfied customers who brag, irate wives who lie, retired hookers with selective recall, neighbors, politicians, crusaders, and gossips, all remembering what they want to remember and elaborating enough to make the facts conversationally interesting.

The Chicken Ranch is fact, fiction, myth; it has engendered innuendos, sympathy, disgust, and self-righteousness. One's perspective is determined by the mood of the moment or the mood as remembered. Let historians sift through abstracts and deeds; the humanist wanders through memories.

The Chicken Ranch

[1]

The Oldest Profession: Facts and Fiction

Writers of fiction have drawn some of literature's most interesting characters from the ranks of prostitution; John O'Hara's *Butterfield Eight*, Steinbeck's *Cannery Row*, and Robert Mason's *The World of Suzie Wong* are American classics that have mined this rich vein. More prostitutes have received fictional immortality than any other class of working girl, and, perhaps it *is* unfair that the "good" girls in other traditionally female occupations have not been given their fair share of the heroines' roles. Nurses and teachers might be considered more worthy and deserving of recognition because their services are more humanitarian.

That, of course, is open to debate.

Artists and writers have appreciated the sensitivity and beauty of the prostitute, attributes that are expounded upon in portrayals of these girls by Steinbeck and O'Hara, whose warm, subtle portrayals are in marked contrast to the cold and crude depictions presented by lesser talents. Two nonfiction accounts, *Hustling* and *The Prostitution Papers*, by their very realistic nature, have been embellished with the romanticism or sensationalism of fiction, but they are regional in scope. A New York hooker has as much in common with a Texas whore as she has with a Carmelite nun.

The world's oldest profession has been such a popular subject for so many books, plays, and movies, that it seems impossible there could be anything original left to say. Famous madams have loved seeing their own names in print and "Memoirs" from Polly Adler, Xaviera Hollander, Pauline Tabor, and others have given everyone—with the price of a paperback—a voyeuristic peep inside a genuine working house. In addition, the news media has kept us abreast, so to speak, on the progress and pitfalls encountered by the ladies in the trade. Any mention of names such as Adler, Hollander, Stanford, Everleigh, and Kimball is sure to ring a bell; would the names of the Supreme Court justices be recognized as quickly? Unfortunately, no.

Journalists, in general, have given the hooker a bad press. When required to write a story about a prostitute, the reporter falls back on a stereotypical version rather than forming an original opinion by direct communication with the subject. If, for instance, both a prostitute and a secretary were to kill their respective lovers, the reporter covering the story on the secretary would be forced to interview the subject or her close associates in order to write an accurate profile. But, on the prostitute's story the work would be cut to a minimum since the "profile of a prostitute" could be pulled from a newsroom file.

At least the professional journalist *thinks* his writing is accurate and objective. But books by madams and hookers are deliberately distorted "inside" stories more injurious to their trade than any news copy. These "inside" revelations and exposés would not sell too well if they portrayed the average whorehouse routine or the average whore. Instead, the authors dwell on the few freaky, far-out misfits they have known, expand upon a few sensational occurrences either experienced or heard, or describe a few sick clients with weird fetishes. Then they spice up the whole thing with a few perversions, add a generous helping of erotic fantasies, and usually sell thousands of books liberally laced with sensationalism. Books that should be called fiction are passed off as "fact" obtained straight from the whore's mouth.

If these "inside" accounts were indeed factual, the heroines would be a rather sorry lot. The hookers' ranks are composed of women from every social, racial, religious, and economic group in North America. Metropolitan areas have a large concentration of prostitutes from the minority groups, but they are less prevalent in the southern and midwestern states. Segregation is still the norm in American prostitution. Houses made up of girls from a particular racial group will usually cater only to their own kind.

Prostitutes frequently come to the trade from conditions of poverty and ignorance. The reasons for a poor girl's entering the life of a hooker are readily apparent. She has not been educated or trained to earn a living in a conventional manner, she has none of the social graces and is easily intimidated by those of superior education or intelligence. Although not as flagrantly apparent, adolescent and preadolescent sexual experiences have also influenced a great number of girls in their limited choice of a "career."

Incest is a repulsive word, but only to those who know its definition. It is merely a fact of life in much of the impoverished and illiterate strata of American society. The incidents of reported incest are infinitesimal compared to the actual incidents of occurrence. It is a "family affair" in every sense of the word. For many of the victims prostitution is a step up. They get paid for doing the same thing they had previously been beaten for not doing.

A book describing the actual facts of life in a brothel *might* result in a best seller, but it would not be a very glamorous or erotic book. In fact, it would not even be sexy.

An instinct for survival has caused most prostitutes and madams to keep a low profile with limited communication outside their own closed society. Their self-imposed isolation is frequently broken by forays into straight society, but they do not admit their profession openly and are consequently accepted by the straights as one of their own. She may be the housewife next door or the nice lady in the neighboring seat at the last PTA meeting. If she does not fit the stereotype, she is above suspicion. Only women in the lowest socioeconomic class can admit having a personal acquaintance with a working prostitute. Other women think they have never met one. They are wrong, of course.

The inadequate communication, negligent journalism, and prejudicial attitudes that perpetrated the unfair stereotyping of the Jews, blacks, and Italians has been recognized and is being dealt with. Prostitutes have also been victims of this same injustice.

There's a great deal left to be said about the world's oldest profession, much more than could be encompassed in one book, and it will not be attempted here. The focus here is directed solely toward one establishment.

There has never been a whorehouse as unique as the Chicken Ranch, nor have there been madams on a par with Miss Jessie and Miss Edna (who had been content to be madams rather than aspiring authors).

Many Texas brothels have gained national fame; Tana Wallace had a well-known brothel in San Antonio in the 1930s, which, some years later, she was forced to move outside of the city limits and disguise as a poodle kennel. The Port Arthur house of Grace Woodyard made her one of the city's wealthiest citizens, a fact that neighboring Beaumont was grateful for after she loaned that city $30,000.00 to pay a delinquent utility bill. Marcella was another infamous Port Arthur madam who was forced into retirement by the Texas Rangers at the same time that they closed down all the houses in Galveston; and, in the capital city of Austin, Hattie Valdez had more politicos sleeping in her beds than the Driskill Hotel could ever boast.

Every city had its red-light district. Dallas had Deep Elm Street and Galveston had Post Office Street. Matamoras Streets in San Antonio was the largest red-light district in the United States during the early years of World War II, but when *Life* magazine ran a feature story, complete with pictures, on the pleasures to be found in the Alamo City, indignant mothers imagined Junior enjoying the War a bit too much. Aghast at all this sinning, they flew into action to save Junior from the whores and managed to close down the whole district. Junior could have learned a few lessons from mama about meeting the enemy head on.

Texas still has plenty of sex for sale. Seedy massage parlors, expensive call girls, and streetwalkers often give a client a screwing, literally and figuratively, but the old-fashioned brothel has gone the way of the buggy whip. The few still in existence are regarded with nostalgic affection.

[2]

Fayette County: Manners, Morals, and Mischief

The nation's oldest continuously operating whorehouse opened for business in 1844, five years after the first lots had been sold in the city of La Grange, Texas. The business operated out of a small, pine-board hotel during its early years, but its location changed at least a half-dozen times during its history. It has been known by several different names, usually the name of its reigning madam. During its final years it was known officially as Edna's Fashionable Ranch Boarding House. This was the name shown on the tax returns, but to several generations of Texas citizens and a large number of other people who had never set foot in the state of Texas it was affectionately known as the Chicken Ranch.

In their first election the citizens of Fayette County, Texas, elected William Nabors to the office of County Sheriff. It was under his watchful eye that the first pioneer "ladies of pleasure" set up business, an alliance with local law enforcement officers that would continue for more than 130 years, through the tenure of Sheriff Nabors, Sheriff J. Moore (elected in 1852), and others. In 1894 August Loessin was elected to the office and served until 1920, at which time he was replaced by his brother Will Loessin, who remained in office until 1946. Sheriff T. J. (Jim) Flournoy was elected in that year and still serves as Sheriff of Fayette County today. Each successive sheriff inherited the office—along with the brothel—from his predecessor. Sheriff Flournoy said, "It's nevrah caused no trouble round here. I ain't nevrah got no complaints." These are the same sentiments expressed by those who had preceded him in office.

Back in 1844 laws were few and enforcement rare. The open

range and unfenced cattle were the spoils of the victor. The victors
of the era had even less regard for the law than the losers, which
probably accounts for their being victors. Murderers, thieves,
drunkards, and the degenerate outcasts of more civilized societies
metamorphosed, with the aid of guns and the acquiescence of the
law, into cattle barons, land owners, and the vanguard of today's
oil magnates. The robber barons, the Mafia, and other assorted
racketeers have received more than ample publicity regarding their
aid and abetment by elected representatives of the law. But their
success is no more attributable to their political influence than that
of the early Texas businessman (and, unfortunately, many of them
today). The aid and abetment is not referred to as such; it is called
"compromisation", a prerequisite for any law enforcement officer
in the south, and especially in Texas. County Sheriffs in the Lone
Star state are past masters in the art of chicanery and diplomacy.

The citizens of Fayette County have demonstrated a remarkable
talent for self-government and a stability in their political
philosophy. Opposition to change has returned the same elected
officials to office year after year; negligence, indiscretion, and even
criminal malfeasance do not necessarily drive a Texas politician
from public office. Texans have always had a glorious rapport with
those public servants whose interpretation of the law was based on
personal preference. A wise choice, perhaps. A less charitable
attitude would have afflicted the state with a dire lack of leader-
ship. Since the days of the Republic the majority of elected officials
and appointed delegates have been men with enough courage to do
the wrong thing when necessary (and sometimes just for the hell of
it).

Texans have always been tolerant of the foibles and faults of
their politicians. There will be respect, not ridicule, for those who
know how to live with this unwritten code, and they will be
returned to office as long as they confine their activities within its
boundaries. The office of county sheriff is in the lower echelon of
political achievement, but cultivation of its representatives has
been pursued on an epic scale. The salary of the office is not on a par
with its influence and prestige. However, the *potential* power and
monetary rewards for the officeholder has no bounds.

The ability to compromise, cheat, coerce, and swindle may be
dubious talents but they are also prerequisites for most Texas

politicians. "Compromisation" is an art; it can be as subtle as Plato's rhetoric or as brutal as a load of buckshot. To outfox a sucker is admirable, to negotiate with an enemy is common sense. "Work hard, play hard, and mind your own business" sums up the credo and philosophy of the folks in Fayette County. The Madams of La Grange understood all of this very well.

Although prostitution is illegal in Texas, each election day gave Fayette County voters the option of deciding whether or not the Chicken Ranch would be allowed to remain open. Had indignant citizens demanded a "cleanup," aspiring office holders would have been happy to grab the ball and run with it, but none received the call. Voters in Fayette were happy with the status quo, and if the assumption is made that the male voters were in the majority and their sympathetic and self-serving vote assured the continued existence of the local whorehouse, this assumption would be wrong. Except for a small number of blue-haired matrons, female voters were not opposed to the Chicken Ranch. Frontier tolerance is still prevalent and contributed to the lack of opposition. So did veneration for the institution. Somewhere along the way the Chicken Ranch changed from a brothel to an inviolable shrine and a tourist attraction. The citizens of La Grange consider the basic commodity and business operation of the Chicken Ranch about as wanton and debauched as Hajovsky's local laundromat.

Neither the blame nor the glory of this venerable establishment lies with any *one* person; tolerance and the desire to just "git along" has prevailed through several generations of merchants, clergy, politicians, and voters. But, it takes more than complacency to elevate a country cathouse to the exalted status attained by the Chicken Ranch. To understand the transformation requires a knowledge of the land and its people, a society influenced by its friends and enemies, and molded by battles won and lost.

Since the closing of the Chicken Ranch, there is not much reason for a stranger to linger in La Grange. The chamber of commerce touts Monument Hill, bringing history buffs, Women's Clubs, and bored senior citizens to visit the memorial to Texas' early heroes, to stroll through quiet neighborhoods, and to picnic under ancient live oak trees. They shop in simple country stores where new spittoons and coal oil lamps are cheap and plentiful. Of course, these are the same items found in Houston, one hundred miles to the east, where the label reads "antique" and is priced accordingly. The visitors also find hearty meals of enormous proportions, and, if there be any truth to the old homily about cleanliness being next to Godliness, every motel proprietor in La Grange can be assured of a place in Heaven.

Visitors will not find strip joints, hippies, hookers, porn shops, rapists, muggers, or perverts. There is a town drunk, a hermit, and a couple of eccentric old spinsters, but that is about as weird as they come in this small country town whose quiet serenity belies its history of conflict and controversy.

It appears that when God finished making the Gulf of Mexico, He rolled out about eighty miles of coastal plain, then abruptly threw up some hills and sprinkled them with hardwood trees to halt the advance of the grasslands. Conflicts between opposing forces have been common occurrences ever since.

Folks in Fayette have always appreciated a good fight. As addicts to conflict, they have always made every effort to join in a good fracas. It did not matter if it pertained to them; it did not even matter much if they agreed with the cause in whose name they were fighting. In fact, they did not even need a cause!

During the Civil War, when young men everywhere were conscripted for military service, the wild youths of Fayette County were itching to go kill some Yankees. Had the voters of Texas decided against secession from the Union, the young warriors from Fayette would have been just as ready and eager to kill Rebels. They were anxious for a fight—any fight. One Company of Fayette County volunteers had six soldiers killed—before they ever saw battle! For lack of a better enemy, they fought each other.

Fayette County has had volunteers eager to fight in every war since the incubation of the Republic. This claim is, of course, familiarly redundant in chamber of commerce rhetoric throughout the State. But in Fayette County the boast has been given visible emphasis. Per capita, the town of La Grange has more monuments to heroes than any other place in North America. The most famous monument is the one on Monument Hill dedicated to the memory of the men in the Dawson and Mier Expeditions and their courageous fight for Texas Liberty; the newest monument honors Sheriff T. J. (Jim) Flournoy, courageous defender of the Chicken Ranch.

To know a given group of people requires knowing their friends, and, especially their enemies. It is not one's friends, but one's enemies who create responses, prejudices, superstitions, and a whole host of habitual reactions and attitudes. People may be known by the friends that they keep, but they are shaped by the foes that they have encountered and Fayette has always been blessed with an abundant supply of antagonists.

The first were the Indians. The noble Red Man. He lived in harmony with nature and the elements, strong of heart and fleet of foot; they were race of people with honor and courage who were inexcusably annihilated by the corrupt and vicious white man. That's what Marlon Brando wants you to believe. In Texas there was another breed of cat.

When the first white man settled in Fayette County in 1821, the tribe in residence was the Tonkawa. The "Tonks," as they were called, were a branch of the Carankawas and were only slightly more enlightened than these primeval cousins. Tonks had most of the bad characteristics of their brethren tribes and a noticeable lack of the good ones. They were chronic beggars by inclination with an innate belief in public ownership of mobile property, preferably on four legs. Their proficiency in the art of horse thievery made them thoroughly hated by the white man and helped hasten the tribe's eventual extinction.

The Indians of the United States had never reached the high degree of civilization that the Toltecs, Incas, and Aztecs had achieved. Civilization has progressed through three periods: the Stone Age, the Bronze Age, and the Iron Age. But the Indians of the United States went directly from the Stone Age to the Iron Age; they were still on the arrow standard when the white man arrived in North America. The Indian's rapid cultural transition after 1492 accounts, at least in part, for their limited intelligence and lack of character.

Contrary to public belief, the Indian was a sorry shot with bow and arrow. There were few exceptional marksmen; the general run of bow-benders had limited accuracy and penetration. Their crude arrows were much too heavy and totally out of proportion. The deviations in the size of the shaft made accuracy in aiming strictly a matter of luck. And to compound the defects in his product, the Indian's fondness for feathers resulted in lavishly decorated arrows that caused a considerable reduction in speed; the feathers merely served as a brake. They could have added one feather up front for stabilization, something European bowmen had learned to do centuries earlier, but that must have been an accomplishment of the Bronze Age, which the Indians had skipped.

This lack of hunting equipment combined with their own natural laziness often left the Tonks without food. This was easily rectified, however, because the Tonks had no qualms about eating humans, preferably enemies but often members of their own group. The Tonks had a sufficient number of enemies to keep their larder full. The Northern Indians had long considered the beautiful hills and valleys of Fayette County their resort area and paid frequent visits spawning frequent battles with the Tonks who were local residents. After the white man settled the area these visits continued by the light of the moon. The visitors stole everything they could lay their hands on and thus accelerated their own extermination.

Individual guilt or innocence was not a consideration when the white man started killing Indians; the familiar credo, "The only good Indian is a dead Indian" went undisputed in Fayette County as long as the Indian remained visible.

A redheaded giant named Aylett (Strap) Buckner was the type of white man with which these doomed Indians had to contend. Strap had a wide reputation as duelist, Indian fighter, and all-around hell-raiser and spent a good deal of time living up to it. He was also playful as a puppy and rambunctious as a rhino in rut. Many a friend was the sorry recipient of a jovial thump on the back that made him a candidate for the hospital or the grave. Strap knocked men down with no intention of doing them any harm; when he joined a group of men they were apt to be bowled over like so many ninepins. But, if any showed blood or bruises, Strap was instant remorse. He would take them to his own bed and have Snoball, the ancient gray-headed black woman who shared his house, nurse them back to health. He would knock them down again as soon as they were fully recovered. According to legend, this gamboling goliath tumbled over the entire male population of Austin's colony at least three times, including Stephen F. Austin, the idolized father of Texas himself.

Fayette County had its first permanent white settler when Strap arrived from Virginia sometime around 1813. Although he is included in the membership of Austin's "Original Three Hundred," Strap actually had taken up squatter's rights along the Colorado River more than nine years before Stephen F. Austin and his colony arrived on the scene.

There was instant dislike between Austin and Buckner, each the antithesis of the other. After several years of hostility, threats, and counterthreats, the two men agreed to compromise their differences; each had something the other desperately needed. Austin had land grants for Buckner, and Buckner had the ability to kill Indians, an innate talent that Austin had not been blessed with. Buckner's reputation as an Indian fighter had grown in esteem during the year of 1826 when he single-handedly surprised and killed thirty Carancawas in retaliation for the murders of the Flowers and Cavanaugh families.

But killing Indians was not a full-time activity. The corporeal pleasures of life have always been of utmost importance to the folks of Fayette, and even during the early, hazardous days of Texas's infancy physical gratification had a priority ranking only slightly below that of physical survival.

The first brewery in Texas was built in La Grange, and the state *is* interested in purchasing that piece of real estate as a historical sight. Most of the counties in Texas have, at some point in their history, voted in favor of temperance; the voters in Fayette County have never voted "dry."

One of the first landowners in the City of La Grange was James Seaton Lester, one of the founders of Baylor University, a devout Baptist and the first man in Fayette County granted a license to sell whiskey. The Lester Hotel, which is still standing at 160 West Colorado Street, was a typical frontier hotel during the 1800s; its barroom produced more revenue than its bedrooms. The Lester Hotel was also a house away from home for no small number of "fancy ladies" during its heyday and was known to every drummer in the south for its "hospitality."

The Original Three Hundred families in Stephen F. Austin's colony were of Anglo-Saxon heritage. The English names of Ross, Powell, and Cummins are still found in Fayette County today. But, they are grossly outnumbered by the German and Bohemian names of settlers who followed in their wake, and it was these latecomers who established the tone and character of the community. The first German settlers came to Fayette County in 1831 and went straight to the business of acquiring huge tracts of land. Entire communities originally settled by Austin's colonizers were eventually bought up by the German immigrants.

In 1840 the congregation of the Fayette County Methodist Church received a charter and a land grant to establish the village and college of Rutersville. A clause in the deed prohibited the sale of "ardent spirits and gambling." Although the college continued to function until the Civil War, it was in hostile territory long before that. By 1856 the original American settlers in the village had sold out to the Germans, leaving the college to be surrounded by the buyers and sellers of the evil "ardent spirits."

The Americans admired the German immigrants for their ambition and thrift, but found them much too coarse, crude, and boisterous. The Germans considered the Americans arrogant, lazy, extravagant, and foolish. These attitudes did not build a close friendship between the two groups; the Americans had a patronizing attitude toward the Germans, and the Germans held themselves aloof from the Americans.

When the Bohemians arrived in 1856 they too found themselves in a class apart from the original Americans for the same reasons the Germans had found this distinction. A natural rapport between the two groups of immigrants was cemented by similiar goals and life-styles, and, perhaps, because they were both shunned by the "elite." But the elite were in the minority and the immigrants soon dominated everywhere; they became merchants, lawyers, landowners, and politicians. The first Bohemian elected Mayor of a United States city was elected in La Grange in 1875.

The immigrants' independence, devotion to hard work, and their genuine delight in earthy amusements were the ingredients that made Fayette County unique. Even though the more genteel Americans did not participate in or appreciate the robust ribaldry of the European immigrants, they were not adverse to sharing in some of their pleasures. The Anglos acquired a taste for the floor-jarring polkas and the "Oompa-Pa" music, but found the bawdy, frequently gross humor and sexual mores of their neighbors abhorrent. The Americans had the traditional Puritan attitude toward sex, which ranged somewhere between "distasteful" and "necessary." At any rate, their preferences were a far cry from the insatiable carnal pleasure enjoyed by the lusty Europeans.

Aside from their native language, the biggest difference between the Bohemian and German cultures was religion. Most Germans were Protestant (usually Lutheran) and the Bohemians were Catholic. Each was convinced that the other was on a straight course to hell and in an intimate league with the devil. The language barrier, in addition to religious intolerance, made social communication between the groups difficult and a clannish nature prevailed for many years.

However, intolerance of another's religion does not preclude tolerance for another's sins. Everyone was tolerant of the bordello in La Grange and was willing to share in its delights with amiable good humor and neighborly affection; there is no communication problem in a whorehouse. Also, both religious groups had been freed from the burden of guilt through the ideology of their own churches. The Catholic could feed his lecherous appetite and be concerned only temporarily about the welfare of his soul or God's eternal wrath. The trick was to live until confession when all would be forgiven. The Protestants of German descent did not find anything that they enjoyed to be sinful in the first place! They were pioneer proponents of the hippie slogan, "If it feels good, do it!"

The open acceptance and tolerance of prostitution in La Grange can be attributed to the influence of the Germans. As any fan of *Cabaret* knows, the Germans have always been delightfully decadent. Their sex is clinical and carnal without the sophisticated naughtiness of Paris; fraüleins lack the flair for sensual showmanship so artfully mastered by their sisters in France. Even in whoring, the Germans are known for their control and discipline, something that has been carried to a rather ridiculous extreme in Germany today. In Frankfurt, one of Germany's largest cities, the red-light district has been cleared of the girls who once chose to live there and has been replaced by the huge metropolitan community of Eros City, a walled compound encircling all of the buildings and shops incidental to any large community. There are also huge high-rise apartments inhabited exclusively by prostitutes. Eros City was created and is devoted entirely to the pursuit or exploitation of commercial sex. By comparison, the Chicken Ranch had more in common with a nursery school.

Although prostitution is no more prevalent in the southern

states than in the northern, it has always found its greatest degree of acceptance below the Mason-Dixon line. Sociologists have attributed this attitude to the heritage of slavery, the relationship between master and slave, with the Negro woman regarded as sexual chattel. After the Civil War this relationship was handily transferred to the white woman and labeled "male chivalry." Only in recent years has it been recognized as the male chauvinism that it has always been.

The sociologists' master/slave theory has some credence, but the Southern "acceptance" was probably closer to "resignation." The high ratio of illiteracy and the poverty of southern whites made prostitution more acceptable than starvation. The red-light district of Baltimore, Maryland, was Mecca to thousands of illiterate coal miners' daughters from Appalachia. And, while it was accepted that poor southern girls would go to a brothel, it was also accepted that nice southern girls didn't ever "put out." Rich girls stayed home and got married and then "put out" occasionally, but only as their wifely duty. Prior to the sexual revolution in the 1960s southern belles were the most neuter members of the human race and their husbands frequently found solace and comfort at the local whorehouse, which, under the circumstances, was considered as necessary to basic community needs as the hospital or police station.

The creators and heirs of Fayette County were an amalgamation of humanity blended from a variety of ethnic, social, and religious legacies; the frontiersman, the German, the Bohemian, and the Southerner constituted a blend of people unique in their morals and actions. They are still an independent people unconcerned with fads or popular opinions. They have evolved standards compatible with their own convictions and ways of life.

Any structure needs proper support to keep from falling and the Chicken Ranch could not have survived to the hoary age of 130 years without the loyal support of friends in Fayette. However, they were just supporters of the structure. Someone else had built it.

[3]

Frontier Bordello: Mrs. Swine and the 'Piglets'

La Grange was a typical frontier town in 1844, blessed with the same number of drunkards, gamblers, whores, and thieves as any other town of the era. Certainly more than one madam set up shop in the new town, but only one has been remembered, for the simple fact that she was so incredibly ugly. She may not have been the first proprietress of America's oldest continuously operating whorehouse, but she is the one remembered. Consequently, one of the most unsightly harridans ever called "madam" has been credited with founding the brothel that would flourish for well over a century.

Her physical and psychological resemblance to a pig was uncanny. Dwarfish arms protruded from her short, squat body; a wide-nostriled nose tilted up toward tiny black eyes peeping out through folds of fat; and her mouth, the most distinguishing part of her ugliness, had a horrible overbite and a hoarse voice that barked orders in an unintelligible combination of English, German, and Yiddish. Little wonder she was known by the sobriquet, "Mrs. Swine."

Or, it may have been personal habits rather than appearance that earned her the name. She arrived in La Grange in a filthy woolen dress of widow's black. She might have owned more than one black woolen dress made in the same pattern, but if this were so they were all equally spotted and gravy-stained. Since longsleeved-woolen garments are not always compatible with the Texas climate, she usually was surrounded by a cloud of pungent odor whose ripeness was noticeable even in this frontier town, where bathing was a frivolous luxury seldom indulged in by anyone.

Mrs. Swine always wore a black hat perched precariously over a huge bun of oily black hair. The hats, always black, were over-decorated with bits and pieces of crumpled ribbons and dusty lace. In the winter she would strut like a queen in an enormous moth-eaten fur coat of dubious original source. Mrs. Swine made many futile concessions to female vanity, but the large diamond ring buried between the fatty mounds of her stubby fingers was the only recipient of admiration and envy.

Three homely young women, all rather thin and pale, had accompanied Mrs. Swine on her move to La Grange from the wicked and sophisticated city of New Orleans, where they had obviously been out of their element. In the rough and primitive village of La Grange the competitive odds were better; courtesans did not seek love and adventure on the frontier—whores did.

Few nineteenth-century prostitutes were the coquettish maids of easy virtue or low moral standards so often portrayed in romantic fiction. Sadly, the majority were pitiful creatures, and victims of social and physical inequities. Many were retarded, tubercular, or syphilitic, and most were illiterate. The proverbial prostitute with a heart of gold was as scarce as the hair in Caesar's beard. Actually, they had nothing of their own to give away, not even their own bodies; they were in complete bondage to the madam.

Although the madam has suffered the contempt of polite society, the nineteenth-century model did deserve a measure of respect and appreciation. She did provide a vital, if unintentional, humanitarian service by harboring homeless, starving, and often contagiously ill young women. The madam took in the most destitute of humans and asked only for their services in return. Unfortunately, the only service they were capable of performing happened to be morally unacceptable, but the morally indignant were slow in providing a better alternative. The madam's reputation has always suffered, perhaps too much. She may have been a Good Samaritan; at least, a necessary evil.

The average pioneer woman was fortunate to live past her thirty-fifth year; the prostitute rarely saw her twenty-fifth. Both the "good" and the "bad" often died from complications of pregnancy and childbirth; the "bad" were also victims of primitive abortions, diseases, and murders.

Tillie was a mentally retarded child of fourteen when she arrived in La Grange under the "care and guidance" of Mrs. Swine. Although she had been cruelly debased, exploited, and abused by the madam, Tillie was entirely devoted to and dependent upon her. Tillie was often the butt of sadistic pranks and was terrified pathetically by tales of witches, werewolves, and Indian atrocities, which sent her running to cower beneath the madam's dirty black skirts, convulsed in fear. In innocent oblivion, Tillie performed the most vulgar sexual perversions while the Madam enjoyed the cruel spectator sport as much as her patrons.

Mrs. Swine was delighted with Tillie's ability to entertain, which was an added attraction in any bawdy house. Nineteenth-century brothels often featured freaks, the unfortunate girls with physical handicaps or grotesque deformities. Folklore has preserved the names: "One-Legged Mary," "Deaf Eddie," "Blind Nellie," "Dummy," "Three-Finger Sally," "Bald Betty" and others. Their handicaps were exploited by the madams in exchange for bed and board. Despicable it was, but life in a brothel was superior to incarceration in one of the overcrowded and disease-ridden public institutions of the era. The odds were against surviving much beyond puberty in either place, but the brothel did offer "living"; there was human contact and communication, affection (of a sort), and even a surrogate mother and family. Furthermore, the handicapped and the extremely young girls were certainly not kidnapped by the madam; the girls were placed in her talented hands by their own "loving" families who either could not, or would not, care for them.

When Mrs. Swine and her bedraggled trio arrived in La Grange, the small town on the banks of the Colorado River was growing fast and had a promising future. In 1838 the Congress of Texas had created Fayette County, with La Grange as the county seat. The rough-shod feet of men and horses had packed the sandy-loam streets as hard as concrete. But, when it rained a small child could have been lost in the deep wagon ruts cut and kneaded in the quagmire.

A few merchants split pine logs to provide a boardwalk down

Main Street and around the square, but each provided only for the front of his own business establishment. Most of the early business-men did not consider customer convenience or civic improvements an obligation needing urgent attention and the boardwalk was built by fits and starts. For many years it resembled a line of Morse code: – – – . . – – . . . . – . Hotels and dry goods stores had boardwalks for the convenience of the ladies; "ladies" were not customers in the other establishments, where the only evidence of concession to customer convenience was a rail where he could hitch his horse. Any lady trying to keep her skirts above the mud of the streets was heady entertainment for the local gawkers too shy or too poor to patronize Mrs. Swine's.

There were also saloons; not a few saloons but many saloons, an overabundance of saloons! At one time in its early history La Grange had so many saloons that every merchant in the business district had two for neighbors, one on each side!

La Grange also had several hotels, inns, taverns, and boarding houses, each as important to the community as they were to the traveler. They provided food and shelter to rural families who traveled many miles to attend Sunday church services, they served as post offices, news headquarters, and social clubs. Some were rowdy and disreputable; others were sedate and refined. All were overcrowded and dirty.

Mrs. Swine took lodgings in one of the crudely constructed hotels in the business district conveniently close to a madam's best referral source, the saloons. The small hotel's twelve rooms in-cluded a public parlor, a dining room, and a barroom, each with a large fireplace, plus as many small bedchambers as space would allow.

The room that Mrs. Swine shared with the girls under her tutelage was as plain as the Madam herself and almost as ugly. Two beds with straw ticks resting on bedcords dominated the tiny room. A washstand with a chipped bowl, a pitcher and accom-panying "towls," a cowhide bottom chair, and a chamberpot summed up the hotel's attempt at furnishings. Mrs. Swine's enormous trunk, with its heavy brass locks, served as a table and conversation piece. The key to the trunk, which hung from an unctuous black ribbon, nestled deep in the fetid furrow between

Mrs. Swine's breasts. Since no one had ever been witness to a "trunk opening," speculation on its contents was as rampant and ridiculous as the conspiracies to gain access to its innards.

No room or bed was private in a frontier hotel and travelers were accustomed to sleeping "nose to nose and toes to toes" with complete strangers—also with bedbugs and lice, who were not strangers. All hotels were on the "American Plan," and competitive innkeepers used the dining room bill of fare as bait to lure new guests. Consequently, all hotels offered meals of gross proportions, usually plain and unimaginative, but always filling.

The whores of 1844 were not streetwalkers, but they were fond of strolling around the square with the madam always squarely in the lead. On Sundays the madam and her girls would dress in their finest regalia and hire an open carriage to drive through the streets. This gave the good ladies of the town an opening to preach indignant sermons on morality to their children, and fathers had a chance to inspect new additions to the merchandise.

Mrs. Swine and her girls led rather dull, socially limited lives, very similar in many respects to the lives of the proper young ladies of the town. They shared a room for sleeping and entertaining callers, but leisure hours were spent in the hotel's sitting room engaged in genteel pursuits and pleasures such as needlework and reading, while at the same time displaying their availability. Callers could make a leisurely appraisal of each girl and her most obvious assets and then, if interested, quietly settle the financial arrangements with Mrs. Swine in exchange for the key to her room. The young woman of his choice would allow several minutes to pass before following at a discreet distance.

The plain young woman, who was so different from the painted ladies or dance hall harlots of places either more sophisticated or rowdy, would participate in a swift and joyless coupling. Neither partner would remove any more clothes than was absolutely required to carry through the task at hand. She was a receptacle for semen, and that was all. Nothing more was extended nor expected. A preferred position was "he on bottom, she on top," she facing either front or back. This took the least amount of effort, time, and disrobing, and allowed both participants to preserve an illusion of modesty. He probably considered this position extremely erotic—especially if the man were married. Good wives of the day considered any deviation from the missionary position to be perverted hedonism.

Occasionally, a drunken farmer or cowhand might dispense with the proper formalities and some unkempt and churlish boors were strangers to protocol and good manners, but their patronage was rarely refused. Mrs. Swine merely adjusted the price to compensate for any insults and affronts to her dignity and to penalize them for their lack of etiquette and finesse.

Today's "account executive" was the "drummer" of 1844; then, as now, the traveling salesman was a hooker's favorite customer. Generally he had more cash money than most callers; he was generous, and he could frequently be coaxed into rummaging through the treasure trove of trinkets in his sample case to select a gift for his favorite girl of the moment.

Drummers were as colorful as peacocks and walked with a corresponding strut. They dressed in the very latest fashion and had all the latest news and gossip plus an inexhaustible supply of jokes and tall tales. Drummers were entertaining, witty, gentle, and kind. They were a whore's favorite customer; they made love with their shoes off.

Drummers and prostitutes had a natural affinity and mutual attraction. A drummer was the innkeeper's most dependable customer and hotels kept prostitutes in residence as a business necessity. Without them the drummers would lodge elsewhere. Besides, the drummers, in their loud suits, bowler hats, and diamond stickpins, were also beguiling bait for prospective hotel guests. They were full of fascinating stories and entertaining antics. Because of their constant travels, the less adventuresome folks considered drummers authorities on almost everything.

War is a marvelous aphrodisiac, and soldiers have always been good customers, but not as consistent as drummers, since wars are only temporary. Mrs. Swine made an astute business decision when she set up shop in La Grange, since Texans were engaged in some type of conflict for years. They fought the Mexicans, fought the Yankees, and occupied their spare time in between and after major scraps by fighting Indians.

Mrs. Swine's stable of working girls was in constant flux. If a girl did not get out of the business at an early age, she could be assured of an early grave. Most girls sought marriage at the earliest opportunity and most found it.

The mortality rate of frontier wives was not much better than it was for frontier whores. Losses to childbirth created a great demand for replacements by widowers whose objective was domestic rather than romantic. It was not unusual for men to outlive three or four wives, burying them in a neat row in the family plot. Young girls were married off as soon as they reached puberty and widowers remarried before their wives' bodies were cold. Some men chose Indian squaws, but a white whore was definitely one notch higher on the social scale. Indians and half-breeds were ostracized by the "good ladies" of the community, but wayward girls who married were accepted as poor lost sheep who had strayed from the fold.

The madam earned a profit even from the marriage of her girls by casting herself in the role of matchmaker. According to custom, she was paid a fee for this service in addition to receiving compensation for the loss of a valuable business asset. Although Mrs. Swine never displayed an increase in material wealth during her many years of business in La Grange, she surely made a fortune from the "rent" and "sale of goods." Only Tillie remained a loyal and devoted employee throughout the years, which remains as mute testimony to her extreme retardation that discouraged even the most destitute of wife-seekers.

The 1850s brought increasing concern about the impending crisis between the North and South over the issue of slavery. The Fayette County citizens were adamantly pro-Union, but the election of Abraham Lincoln to the Presidency caused many residents to do an abrupt about-face. Lincoln was universally and vigorously despised. When news of his victorious election reached La Grange, a black flag was run up on the square.

The issue of secession was brought to a vote on February 23, 1861, and the Fayette County voters defeated the move for secession by a narrow margin of twenty votes. It was the only county in Texas to vote in favor of preserving the Union.

The loyal opposition to secession faded when war was declared. The majority of Fayette County citizens parted with their Unionist convictions and served the Confederacy as faithfully as the original secessionists.

But, that is not to say they all went off to war to do their duty as seen by their government. Those who chose to, went; others stayed home. The German and Bohemian farmers, in particular, refused to be conscripted. They hid in the woods and fields; while some were harrassed, most were ignored. Only six men from Fayette County were sent to Andersonville Prison for refusing to serve with the Confederate Army and inciting the people against the Confederacy. Those who had exercised more discretion in voicing their opinions were not imprisoned. Although some were called traitors, none were called cowards; they had proved their courage in the Indian Wars. In fact, calling the German-Bohemian farmers "traitors" was a slanderous exaggeration; they were merely apathetic toward the war. Their dedicated commitment and total absorption in the land would not be deterred by the frivolous quarrels between opposing ideologists.

The Civil War brought soldiers to La Grange, but the war had drained the county of hard money. Confederate treasury notes depreciated rapidly and the cost of even the simplest, most basic commodities rose exorbitantly. Taxes were levied to aid destitute widows and orphans, but due to the lack of real money the taxes were paid with provisions: corn was redeemable at fifty cents per bushel; bacon, twelve-and-a-half cents per pound.

Mrs. Swine's hasty departure from La Grange during the Civil War was probably spurred on by financial or political difficulties (most likely a combination of the two). She was suspected of being a Yankee sympathizer and accused of being a traitor as well. The camaraderie and rapport between the madam and her customers and friends was gone, replaced with an aura of distrust and furtiveness. It is most unlikely that this insignificant madam of a backwoods brothel had any part to play in the War, but accusations had been made—if not directly, then at least by innuendo— and the fear of Andersonville Prison weighed heavily on her mind.

Mrs. Swine left La Grange wearing a filthy black dress that may have been the same one she wore on her arrival twenty years earlier. The eternally innocent Tillie went with her.

The years of reconstruction were as painful to bear in Fayette as anywhere else in the South. Many returning veterans considered all Confederate property as their own. In May 1865, they named a committee to collect government property in the county and distribute it to indigent veterans and their families. They also pillaged government stores, confiscated anything not openly guarded by its rightful owners, and created mass chaos and confusion.

Union soldiers were brought in to stay until the lawlessness could be brought under control, a task that proved to be both difficult and perplexing to the Yankees. The characteristic disorder of frontier life, the additional lawlessness spawned by the Civil War, and the humiliation of losing that war left a residue of ungovernable renegades in an apathetic society. During the term of Governor Edmund J. Davis (1871–1873) emancipated slaves were given a gun and a badge and appointed to the state police; they terrorized communities, openly murdered whites, and compounded the violence that was already rampant.

This drastically altered atmosphere brought a different class of prostitute to La Grange after the War between the States. She was no longer the demure young lady who sat in a hotel lobby with her needlework, waiting for a customer and longing for a husband. She had changed and so had her customers. Carpetbaggers, scalawags, gunslingers, and the sadistic, unscrupulous lawmen who dogged their steps became the patrons of the prostitute. And, the prostitute became a slut.

Outlaws replaced drummers as the favored clientele. The outlaws' inexhaustible supply of money could buy any favor; none were too vile if the price was right. The crude and vulgar sex of Mrs. Swine's era was merely a primitive pastime when compared to the debauchery of the postwar years.

The raucous and gaudy brothels formed a business alliance with the saloons. Open solicitation became the rule; streetwalking, provocative window posing, and hustling drunks was the modus operandi. It is unfortunate that the traditional reluctance of Texans to record unsavory aspects of their history has obscured the details and the identity of the perpetuators of America's oldest whorehouse during the final decades of the nineteenth century. The frontiersman was struggling toward refinement, and, any impulses to accurately recall ancestral scoundrels were stifled. This, of course, allowed succeeding generations a free hand in the embellishment and aggrandizement of illusive kin. Many a frontier floozy is remembered today as a "great-great grandmother, a charmin' little lady. Charter member of The Daughters of the Confederacy, you know."

[4]

Miss Jessie: From Cottonfield to Chicken Ranch

During the closing years of the nineteenth century the whores of La Grange migrated from the hotels to a red-light district on West Travis Street. There, a dozen or so pineboard shacks lay scattered along the banks of the Colorado River. The shabby appearance of the unpainted, one-room houses was in direct contrast to the appearance of the occupants, nor were the humble dwellings indicative of the profitable business conducted under their eaves. When Jessie Williams arrived in 1905 she found the commerce both lively and lucrative.

Jessie was a professional woman from Waco, Texas, where she had learned her trade, and was obviously successful, since she owned a home in that city when she was less than twenty-five-years-old. She soon owned another along the banks of the Colorado in La Grange.

Jessie Williams had been christened Faye Stewart after her birth on a hardscrabble farm near Hubbard, Texas. Her education was erratic, interrupted by cotton to be picked and turnips to be hoed. A long bout with diphtheria finally put an end to the haphazard education after her sixth year of grammar school and brought an end to cotton chopping chores as well. The long illness had left the young farm girl too weak to be of use in her rural environment or to her family. What is more, farm boys did not come courting a wife if the object of their attention was too puny to handle a hoe.

Faye Stewart moved to Waco when she was fourteen and managed to support herself by finding work as a "hired girl" for local families; board and room was free, sometimes a salary of two or three dollars a week was also paid. But the work was hard, the hours were long, and the chores were tedious. The hours from dawn till dark were filled with laundry, cooking, scrubbing, crying babies, and unruly children; it was month after weary month of boring drudgery and meager rewards.

But Sundays were special. As capital of the Bible Belt, Waco and its God-fearing citizens paid strict observance to the Sabbath; even the lowly hired girl was given a day for rest and worship, for flirting, for gossip, and for promenading round the square to see and be seen. Faye Stewart observed the Sabbath in the expected manner, but there were some unexpected results.

Church services are frequently described as inspiring, but the congregation was Faye's inspiration. They inspired a fervent desire for fancy clothes, for someone to love, for a carriage and team of her own plus a mansion to call home. She studied the habits and manners of the most affluent members of the congregation and copied their speech and affectations. Her daydreams were peopled by rich young bachelors pleading for her hand; her wedding gown was planned down to the last bead, the rooms of her dream house lay sprawled in her head, and she had picked the names for at least one half-dozen fat, healthy babies.

But Faye Stewart was more than an idle dreamer. She was realistic enough to know that she would not attract any wealthy young bachelors, at least not in her present position as a hired girl who had a wardrobe assembled out of the scraps and castoffs of her employers. She recognized her own inadequacies, her lack of education or marketable skills, and her lack of "family," influence, and inheritance. Faye Stewart was also cognizant of her assets, and their limits and limitations. She would make them suffice.

Faye was a small woman slightly over five feet in height, and so thin and pale only her fine bone structure saved her from appearing gaunt. She had large, beautiful eyes (the one thing relatives and friends had always commented on, ever since her childhood), her nose was delicate and straight, her hair was adequate, and her thin waist emphasized an ample bosom.

Her assets were identical to those of the "fancy ladies." And these ladies, who also promenaded on Sunday afternoons, had all the things Faye Stewart's dreams were made of: the most fashionable clothes in all of Waco, perhaps in all of Texas; the teams that pulled their open coaches, or the broughams on inclement Sundays, were matched pairs whose harnesses were always well-oiled and the brass always polished. "Fancy ladies" lived in fancy houses where lamps with enormous colored-glass shades cast soft, golden rays of light over carpets and horsehair sofas, where only black girls washed a dish or scrubbed a floor.

When sick folks died or babies were weaned, the hired girl knew that she had better start looking for other employment. Faye had found herself in this position more than once. However, sick folks and new babies always outnumbered hired girls, and a new family to work for was not difficult to find. A few months before Faye's eighteenth birthday this prospective change of employer and lodgings became imminent once again. This time she would not settle for a bare, stuffy room up under the eaves.

Faye Stewart had no difficulty in finding work and a room of her own in Waco's finest brothel. She was prettier, healthier, smarter, and more refined than any of her co-workers. She was also a virgin, a rare commodity that the madam exploited to its fullest by selling the "de-flowering" at least five times, maybe more.

Faye changed her hair style, her manner of dress, her habits, and her name. Miss Jessie Williams had arrived. Within a few years Miss Jessie owned her own house in Waco, a small and inelegant house with only three girls, but it was *her* house. Regardless, it was a successful and profitable house. Why she chose to leave it for a weathered shanty on the banks of the Colorado River was the subject of much speculation. Family pressure, a thwarted love affair, and threats from competitors were some of the rumored reasons. Miss Jessie never chose to divulge the real reason.

She surely did not leave at the request of the law, because Miss Jessie had become a master at small-town diplomacy, a talent that served her well as a newcomer to La Grange.

The first order of business for madams in a new town had always been to cement relations with local law enforcement officers. With this goal in mind, Miss Jessie sought an alliance with the Loessin brothers. August Loessin was sheriff of Fayette County, and his younger brother Will was chief deputy as well as city marshal of La Grange. (He would succeed his brother August as sheriff of the county in 1920.)

The Loessins were widely known and respected as law officers. Will was an outstanding investigator and gained a statewide reputation for his ingenious detective work. August was just as widely venerated for his courageous victory over the infamous Ku Klux Klan, which had regrouped and gathered strength during the opening years of the twentieth century. Although many central Texas sheriffs opposed the detested Klan, August Loessin was the only sheriff to make a serious, and victorious, effort to rid his county of the organization.

Miss Jessie and the Loessins managed a coexistence that was beneficial and profitable to all parties concerned. She caused the law no trouble or embarrassment, and the law reciprocated by ignoring her existence, something they would have preferred doing with the inhabitants of the other houses along the river bank, but had not been able to do. While Miss Jessie had discouraged drunkards and rowdies from patronizing her house, the other madams and girls on the street had not been as discriminating. Cutting and shooting scrapes were common occurrences; pimps, bootleggers, and runaway youngsters had all taken up squatters rights along the River and were a bothersome nuisance to the city marshal. Each year brought an influx of riffraff and their abominable dwellings. The quarter's frequent house fires were a rather mixed blessing; their close proximity to the downtown business area was certainly a hazard, but they did eliminate many of the wretched hovels. The inhabitants, both human and rodent, usually survived the holocausts to seek shelter in other huts already overcrowded with both.

By 1915 the degenerates' ghetto threatened to engulf the town square. Brothels and bootleggers were doing an open business a half-block from the county jail, while pimps and panderers solicited on the courthouse steps. Improved transportation brought an influx of visitors to La Grange and helped spread the word about its unsavory reputation. The snickers and leers of strangers were far more offensive to the city fathers than the immorality in their midst. Ashamed embarrassment had agitated the clergy and the Daughters of the Confederacy into a "cleanup crusade," something righteous indignation had never been able to accomplish.

Whores, pimps, bootleggers, and other sundry scoundrels were no longer welcome to connive or cavort on the banks of the Colorado. Those who did not leave voluntarily were jailed, pimps were coerced and threatened, and, if still not convinced to leave, an "accidental" death through drowning or fire was arranged to send the reluctant on their final journey. La Grange wanted to be a progressive city and a few ne'er-do-wells were not going to get in the way! To quote George Bernard Shaw, "Men have to do some awfully mean things to keep up their respectability."

Miss Jessie was not sacrificed to the tide of progressive reform. Her well-cultivated friendship with the Loessin brothers saved her and two of her friends from the escorted trip to the train station that had been the fate of others of her profession. Whores were presented with a one-way train ticket and the farewell words, "Don't look back." At least they fared better than the runaway children who were merely shown the way downstream, or the abandoned dogs who were left to forage among the deserted hovels.

Miss Jessie had been informed of the cleanup campaign long before it actually got underway. Her house had offered safe and gracious hospitality to lawmen and politicians when they were neither welcome nor comfortable in other brothels or any number of respectable parlors. Their concern and subsequent acts of toleration regarding Miss Jessie's fate were, therefore, generous, but not entirely altruistic.

With forewarning and help from her contingent of horny, influential friends, Miss Jessie was prepared for the exodus from the river bank. The sale of her real-estate holdings in Waco supplied the cash needed to buy eleven acres and a two-room house outside the city limits, and only two blocks off the busy Houston-Galveston Highway. The property contained another one-room house set among the cedars and oaks. This was moved three hundred yards or so, to become the first of many additions to the original two rooms.

Miss Jessie shared the three rooms—a kitchen, and two bedrooms—with a pleasantly plump young woman named Alma, but she did not waste any time in building on to both the house and the business. In the whorehouse business the number of rooms usually corresponds to the number of girls who work there.

The towns that had sprouted so rapidly in the wake of oil discoveries in East Texas had begun to lose some of their "boom" by 1915. As the fields were established the roughnecks and roustabouts moved on, leaving hundreds of wooden derricks and a brigade of prostitutes behind. The derricks were still utilized, but the prostitutes were not. Many drifted toward the coast and the corrupt debauchery of the seaport towns, while others followed the departing roughnecks, but two freckle-faced young pixies decided to separate from the departing herd. They wanted more from their future than a crib and a cot.

The "Sisters" arrived on Miss Jessie's doorstep in the spring of 1917. They were not the first to seek shelter and employment at the three-room house, but they were the first allowed to stay. Miss Jessie had a couple of rooms tacked on in a casual, haphazard way that would eventually give the house its unique style.

The country belles of La Grange had not mastered all the tricks that the "Sisters" had learned and only few of them were as attractive. Their quality of "wicked, yet cute" made young men feel like sophisticated degenerates and old men like perverted rogues. They loved it!

With her usual commercial acumen, Miss Jessie promoted the "Sisters" to a middle-management position. Customer relations was a prerequisite in their line of work, but it could also be practiced without bodily contact. When the young farm boys of Fayette left to fight in the big war that was to make the world safe for democracy, Miss Jessie and her girls were their favorite pen pals. They mailed cookies and the local papers, knitted the socks, and sent their "Love and xxxxx's." If the "girls next door" got the publicity, the girls from Miss Jessie's did not mind. Prostitutes have no desire for public recognition—not even when their deeds are good ones. One wonders how generous such world-famous philanthropists as Carnegie, Mellon, Ford, Rockefeller, and others of their ilk would have been had they been sworn to anonymity.

As heroines in a dime novel the "Sisters" would have been perfect casting. And, totally in character, they stuck to the plot.

Shortly after the Armistice of 1918, one of the sisterly pair fell in love with one of her customers. He was an older man who was charming, educated, and wealthy. While there is no evidence that he was the originator of the well-worn phrase, "Let me take you away from all this," he must have chosen words to that effect. The two were married and lived together in a stately, old mansion in San Antonio until the old gentleman's death more than thirty years later. The couple had been childless, and the wealthy widow became one of the Alamo City's most beloved benefactors and patron of the arts.

The older sister stayed on at the house in a management position until her death at the age of eighty.

All the old rules vanished in the twenties, and everybody went on a prolonged spree. The characteristic figures of the decades were the flapper and the bootlegger, and they were both in love with the automobile. Westbrook Pegler had called it the "Era of Wonderful Nonsense," but it was also the era of materialism. As old certainties and basic assumptions were abandoned, material goods took their place.

The increase in the number of automobiles brought increased traffic to the nation's highways, which was a real boon for the proprietor of a country whorehouse. Miss Jessie responded by taking in a few more girls and tacking a few more rooms onto the house whose style could be likened most appropriately to a maze.

The decade of rapid changes in society's morals and life-styles had less impact on La Grange than it had on New York City, but even country gals cater to fashion. They bobbed their hair (Miss Jessie was the lone exception), rolled their stockings, smoked cigarettes and small cigars, drank gin, and tooled about in sports cars. When the flapper was in vogue, it was difficult to distinguish the amateur whores from the pros.

Miss Jessie's new affluence brought a horsehair sofa and velvet-covered side chairs to the waiting room along with all the stylish bric-a-brac of that gilded age, including velvets, tassels, and rose-covered carpets (none of it considered "modern" in that sophisticated era). But Miss Jessie's tastes ran to "traditional whorehouse." All that it lacked was a piano; she bought a Victrola instead.

In the age of the roadster business was no longer dependent on the high jinks of local bumpkins on Saturday night or the latest batch of drummers getting off the train. Banker and bank robber, bootleggers and Baptists, all rubbed elbows and shared the merchandise in a brotherly spirit and with such an abundance of sincere generosity that it warmed the heart of every priest and politician in the house.

The influx of new customers that arrived with the auto age was not ignored by Sheriff Loessin. He was not interested in arresting bootleggers—not if he wanted to be reelected in this German-Bohemian community, but he was interested in those customers at Miss Jessie's who were involved in more serious criminal activities.

Since a professional criminal's vocation requires a great deal of travel, and most of it hurried, he is not in a position to make permanent ties or commitments with women. He is, therefore, obliged to buy female relationships, and, while buying a woman's attention and affection may be gratifying, it is also emasculating and accounts for the high incidence of rape when sexual gratification can be purchased so easily. The customer in a whorehouse may feel reassured of his own masculinity through copious copulation, but he also feels required to prove to the woman of the moment that he is more than just a stud. He must impress her with his achievements. This affliction is not limited to the criminal; bankers brag on their foreclosures and priests on their converts. But the criminal's braggadocio on murder and mayhem is often incriminatory, either of himself or his friends.

These squealers in a prone position had Will Loessin's sleuthful soul in ecstacy. Sheriff Loessin had discovered this primitive, but effective, wiretap when Dick Nixon was still in knickers. The sheriff's last chore of every working day was a trip to the house on the outskirts of town to visit with Miss Jessie and the girls, to glean the gossip and rumors that had accumulated during the day. The sexy little tattletales contributed more aid to the sheriff of Fayette County than the Texas Rangers ever had. As a bonus the Sheriff picked up a reputation as a detective par excellence, while Miss Jessie's whorehouse became indispensible to local law-enforcement officers. A bonafide, sealed, and signed "Official Whorehouse Operator's License" from the City fathers would not have served her any better.

The returning heroes of World War I had spread the gospel of cosmopolitan sophistication, yea, even unto the hinterlands of Central Texas. Miss Jessie's girls were as chic as their sisters in Baltimore or San Francisco, their roadsters as shiny, their language as coarse, and their house as flashy as a gambler's stickpin. But progress halted at the bedroom door. Erotic sex was an abomination in Miss Jessie's eyes; a customer wanting anything more imaginative than the basic missionary position was considered some kind of pervert and thrown out of the house. The girls at the farm had welcomed the boys with open arms—and legs, but Miss Jessie's welcome was tempered with suspicion, especially of those who had seen "Paree!" The suspicions were not groundless. These veterans, nee plowboys and cowboys, had sampled the wares around the world and were anxious to demonstrate their continental expertise for the girls back on the farm.

There are no locks on bedroom doors in a whorehouse, which is a necessary precaution against the occasional drunk or sadist, but at Miss Jessie's house it was not the predominant reason. It was Miss Jessie's custom to prowl the halls listening for the alien, telltale sounds of imaginative aberrations that some creative (or bored) customer had added to the limited repertoire of pleasures. Her suspicions adequately aroused, Miss Jessie would crash through the door in a rage of contemptuous anger, swinging a large iron rod at the rapidly fleeing backside of the improvisor.

When the continentally-whetted appetite of one Fayette farmboy (a three-times-a-week regular) hungered for more exotic fare than the locally available merchandise had to offer, his efforts in on-the-job training resulted only in getting him barred from the house for more than a month. He had been trying to explain to a girl named "Deaf Eddie" some intricately pleasurable moves which called for rather elaborately detailed and explicit navigational instructions. The whole maneuver could have come off quite well if it had not been for the girl's hearing problem.

As the customer recalls,

> "See, we called her Deaf Eddie cuz she really wuz harda' hearin' . . . couldn'ta heared herself fart inna churn, so I wuz havin' ta talk purty loud. Well, what happened, Miss Jessie come achargin' in there, ahittin' me with that big ole iron rod and ayellin' at me bout turnin' her girls inta dirty French whores! I grabbed up my pants and made a beeline for the door. Didn't go back for a week. Then she wouldn't let me in! Not till I'd showed her I could be right happy with just your ordinary piece of tail, without exters."

Miss Jessie and her girls had shared in the prosperity of the twenties, and when the market crashed in 1929 the impact was as devastating to Miss Jessie's country cathouse as it was to the firms on Wall Street. There were fewer customers with less to spend, and, simultaneously, there were more girls eager to join the world's oldest profession. After fares were reduced to correspond with supply and demand, the lack of customers was no longer a complaint. In fact, prostitution flourished during the depression years of the thirties. Sociologists have attributed the increase in brothel business during the depression to unemployment. Men who were questioning their own masculinity because of their failure to provide for their families could reaffirm their maleness by visiting a prostitute. They also had the idle time to indulge in these ego trips.

Normal marital relations suffered during this period; many wives discouraged their husbands' sexual advances due to fear of pregnancy, which would result in another mouth to feed when income was already severely limited and frequently nonexistent.

Prostitutes were charging less during the Depression due to general economic conditions, but the bargain rates at brothels were also caused by the many amateurs who had turned professional because of difficulties in finding other employment. The frivolous flappers of the twenties drifted toward obscurity, replaced by the displaced, heavy-hipped frumps from factories and farms.

The panic on Wall Street lost intensity as it spread through the country. Rural America felt its impact, but less keenly so than in urban areas. Hard cash was as scarce in La Grange, Texas, as in New York City, but in an agrarian community people could, and did, live off the land.

Doctors, dentists, lawyers, and preachers were equally short of cash, but they and their families lived and ate well. Farmers and ranchers paid their bills with butter, eggs, vegetables, and meat, while merchants traded goods for produce or services rendered. Few rural Americans experienced the pangs of hunger (for food, that is). Other appetites were not faring so well—Miss Jessie demanded cash.

The price for a "regular date" at Miss Jessie's (and Miss Jessie offered no other kind) was down to $1.50 by 1932, a reasonable rate, but few were buying. Few people had cash, fewer still were willing to part with it.

The prosperity of the twenties had imbued Miss Jessie with the cagey instincts and financial wizardry of a Sharpstown banker, but her "down home" talent for honest horse tradin' was still intact. Hard times brought hard bargaining—Miss Jessie's business converted to the "Poultry Standard"—one chicken for one screw.

Anyone who grew up in the country can see the logic in the solution. If a farmboy did not have a chicken of his own he could always "find" one easily. This was especially true in Central Texas, where most chickens in the thirties were still roosting in the trees. That is not to say a coop was an impregnable fortress guaranteeing safety for the chicken. They were actually easier to catch inside a coop, but they could sure set up an awful racket! That woke the dog that woke the farmer that slept with his double-barrelled shotgun within easy reach, right next to his boots and galluses.

There are some afficianados of Chicken Ranch lore who say the place got its name from all the good-looking chicks who lived there. Chicken Feathers!

The rumor is not only colorless and dull, it is unlikely as well, and should have been put to rest when the huge parking lot sitting in the midst of a large grove of oak trees started filling up with chickens. For a year or two the chippies at Miss Jessie's ate more chicken than a country preacher; the fare was filling—but what a bore!

It was not exactly the U. S. Cavalry that came riding over the hill to save these girls from their dietary doldrums, but the rescue crew was a pretty fair facsimile.

President Franklin Delano Roosevelt has the dubious distinction of instigating the use of initials in lieu of names that we are weary of deciphering today; he gave us TVA, NRA, REA, WPA, and others, including CCC. The CCC translates into Civilian Conservation Corporation. The Federal Government established numerous camps throughout the United States for the jobless young men who had joined the CCC to work in forestry, land conservation, and beautification. (Ecologists, if you will, but the word was not in common usage during the thirties.) Many of the scenic parks and roadways that we are enjoying today are the handiwork of the CCC.

When the CCC built Camp Swift near La Grange Miss Jessie's

fortune and future were given a bracing belt of optimism. Camp followers have been legend throughout history—Hannibal crossed the Alps followed, in order, by 90,000 infantry, 12,000 cavalry, 40 elephants, and 1,000 whores. Twenty-one centuries later the camp came to the girls.

[5]

World War II: G.I. Joes and Ginny

World War II brought back prosperity and a tidal wave of service-men to the state of Texas. The girls at the Chicken Ranch baked the obligatory cookies, wrote V-Mail letters, and literally worked their tails off. While their sisters in the city were coping with the problems of ration stamps by dealing and trading for black-market wares, the girls at the ranch "rode" out the war by subsisting on the still-prevalent chicken and eggs, a side of beef from a satisfied customer, gasoline from local farm boys with an unlimited supply of coupons, and assorted GI staples filched from area mess halls. Although Miss Jessie was confined to a wheelchair by crippling arthritis, she still ruled the house with an iron hand and an iron rod, and coached the girls in their feeble efforts at growing a Victory Garden.

Twenty years earlier a resident of the Chicken Ranch would have needed no coaching in gardening; most of them were farm girls. But the girls at the ranch, like girls everywhere in America, had changed over the decades. Farm girls were fewer, and, in general, girls were prettier, brighter, and better educated. But more than that they had self-confidence, self-assurance, and the poise and self-determination that most women had lacked previously, especially women in a whorehouse. The girls at Miss Jessie's were no longer the guilt-ridden recluses of an earlier era.

Prior to 1940, and contrary to popular belief, "ladies of the night" had not been the attractive creatures portrayed in books and movies; they were usually society's misfits, even before choosing their profession. Prostitutes are still less attractive and intelligent than their "straight" sisters; many are scarred, blemished, or inflicted with a physical deformity. Many can still be classified as mildly retarded. This has been true all through recorded history and is still true today. However, there was a significant improvement in the merchandise after World War II.

Improved health care, education, and communication had brought about changes in the living standards and life-styles of most Americans born after 1920. The advent of radio in 1921 plus the proliferation of "talkies" that followed after *The Jazz Singer* in 1928 brought the manners and morals of all Americans together in a homogeneous blend. The resulting laxity of the moral code helped prostitutes to overcome feelings of fear, guilt, and self-abasement. Prostitution was no longer the refuge of freaks, social misfits, and outcasts who had no other option; the quality of the average whore was upgraded considerably when self-reliant young women entered the profession by choice, free of guilt and a fear of ostracism.

Every whorehouse from Maine to Malibu has had its resident college graduate—at least in fable. In reality, most girls working out of a house do not have a high school diploma, and a few of the girls who worked for Miss Jessie in the forties were downright stupid, but the "doxy with degree" was in residence too.

There were many University of Texas coeds who financed an education by working at the Chicken Ranch during summer breaks. When classes would resume in the fall the girls would return to Austin and their studies at UT, live in a swanky apartment, drive a new car, array themselves in the latest fashions, and act as refined and dignified as any sorority gal on campus. Male students from La Grange would often see their summertime playmates in class at UT; they respected their anonymity, and vice versa.

One of the most accomplished classical musicians in Texas is a striking, raven-haired beauty, now in her mid-fifties, who earned an MA in music with earnings from the Chicken Ranch. Today she lives in isolated seclusion behind the high fence which surrounds her beautiful country estate near Austin. She shares her life and her music only with her husband (her third) and a contingent of Doberman Pinschers. Her clothes, manners, surroundings, and habits are exquisite. A succession of three wealthy husbands has enabled her to live a life of refined elegance on a par with the bluebloods. Some possibly might consider her a courtesan, but only those acquaintances of more than thirty years would find credence in the facts.

Ginny (a fictitious name used for the sake of clarity and the avoidance of lawsuits), is a contradiction of "virtue being its own reward," but she is by no means unique or even rare. The vaguely British accent of her well-modulated voice belies her birth on a central Texas caliche-laden goat ranch. Goat ranchers usually do not send daughters to college.

Ginny's talent at the piano brought her a scholarship to the University of Texas, but that's all that it brought. Sans money, clothes, and all the other accoutrements of taste and breeding, Ginny would have been more content on the goat ranch. Depending on one's point of view her good looks saved her or ruined her; at any rate, beauty brought pay for play. Ginny was an employee of Miss Jessie's for five summers and did no small amount of moonlighting after classes during the rest of the year, occasionally working out of the house of Miss Hattie Valdez in Austin during the school year. It was a very good and appropriate arrangement! The summers at the Chicken Ranch were casual, private, and low-keyed. The winters with Miss Hattie were only an extension of her pursuit for knowledge. Miss Hattie taught her to walk, talk, eat, sit, stand, dress, and, somewhere along the way, threw in a few hints on how to make love. Miss Hattie graduated nothing but ladies.

Ginny married husband number one when she was twenty-nine and he was forty-four. He was wealthy, as were all her husbands, an oilman who spent at least ten months out of every year looking after oil interests outside of the United States. He was a wheeler-dealer in the best Texas tradition even though his interests were in Venezuela rather than the Lone Star state.

During their four-year marriage Ginny took a crash course in "wheeling-dealing" from the master, gave birth to a daughter, had a well-paying affair with a prestigious attorney, and managed to manipulate all of her first husband's assets into the community property category prior to their divorce.

Husband number two followed much the same pattern, except for the fact that his business interests kept him in Paris and he was not presented with an heir. They were married for seven years, and, although she had a bit of trouble converting the assets, the years were not wasted. Although no longer a prostitute or call girl in a manner that those words usually convey, Ginny's business affairs were still being conducted in the bedroom rather than the boardroom. She was still a hustler, only her client did not know he was paying.

Ginny retired just after her fortieth birthday, immediately following the most rewarding coup of her career. An Austin businessman then in his mid-seventies, lonely, bitter, and alienated from his family, sought solace and sex in Ginny's relatively young arms. Hope sprang eternal—among other things long dormant. Within five months Ginny owned title to his home, the overriding royalties on six producing oil leases plus a working interest in three more, became the major stockholder in three corporations, acquired unlimited credit on an assortment of charge cards, secured the cash from several life insurance policies (no longer needed—he was growing younger by the day) and wore the diamonds belonging to his wife who never missed them; she had been confined to a rest home in an advanced state of senility for many years.

Two months after the affair ended the old gentleman was dead, his estate depleted and his sons left with nothing but the bill for his burial.

Ginny shucked husband number two and replaced him with number three, a wealthy man, of course, but also an affectionate man and a homebody. They live extremely private lives behind the high fence and padlocked gate of their country estate where admission is gained only by phoning in advance, and their number is unlisted. Ginny is rich, content, loved, and respected. The wages of sin are sometimes quite liberal.

College coeds were not the only ones paying for an education with earnings from the Chicken Ranch. Many a prominent businessman can thank his sweet wife for the education she earned for him by working in La Grange. While hubby was busy with his classes at the University of Texas in Austin, the "little woman" was entertaining the boys from Texas A & M.

Although their patronage started sometime earlier, it was during the 1940s that the boys from Texas A & M found that being a staunch devotee of the "house away from home" was a mandatory requirement. There were probably hundreds, if not thousands, of freshmen students at A & M who would have just as soon "passed" when offered the pleasures to be found at the Chicken Ranch, but participation was traditional, a ritual. If you wanted to be an Aggie you had to abide by these things!

During the forties most of the residents of Aggieland were boys from the farms and small towns of Texas and its neighboring states. Incoming freshmen who wanted to be farmers, soldiers, or veterinarians were among the most unsophisticated newcomers any campus ever embraced. It is no small wonder that they were so easily enticed by the wicked Lorileis of La Grange, but it would be interesting to know precisely what attracted them; was it curiosity, or was it lust? Perhaps it was the fear of being called chicken.

In 1946 Miss Jessie was in her mid-sixties and confined to a wheelchair by crippling arthritis. Sheriff Will Loessin retired that year, but Miss Jessie, formidable as always despite her physical handicap, had no difficulty in forming an alliance with the sheriff's replacement. Miss Jessie had become an integral part of the community. She had contributed to its churches, its civic organizations, and she had a reputation as an easy mark for any type of charity seeking generous donors. Being the county's most generous philanthropist was an ingenious public-relations accomplishment. The resulting publicity and its effect on public opinion could not have been handled better by an expert in Madison Avenue wizardry.

Although Miss Jessie forbade judiciously any social contact between the girls at the ranch and the residents of La Grange, she did encourage them to shop with the local merchants. On their weekly trek to the County Medical Examiner (an office that the Fayette County grand jury had created solely for their use) the girls would buy candy, clothes, magazines, and cosmetics. And, occasionally, one might buy an automobile.

As an astute practitioner of diplomatic trade relations Miss Jessie made sure that the groceries and other commodities needed at the Ranch were purchased from local merchants on a rotating basis in weekly cycles that were repeated over and over again for many years.

Lester (Buddy) Zapalac, editor of the La Grange Journal, described the lady well, "She just had ta be one of the most amazin' women who ever lived. She was strong! But she was generous too. And whooooh, boy, was she a smart one!"

With foundations laid firmly and relations well-cemented, Miss Jessie anticipated no problems with the new sheriff, T. J. (Jim) Flournoy.

The Ranch itself, on the outskirts of La Grange. (Courtesy Dallas Morning News.)

Edna Milton, newly transformed into Broadway actress, poses out-side the Broadway theater where she appeared in a musical based on her past. The show, "The Best Little Whorehouse in Texas," is the story of the Chicken Ranch, which Edna used to own. She played the small, non-speaking role of her predecessor at the ranch—bringing an earthy touch of real life to the musical's romanticized version of the ranch's closing in 1973. (Courtesy World Wide.)

Sheriff Jim Flournoy. (Courtesy Houston City Magazine.)

Marvin Zindler on the air. (Courtesy Houston Town and Country Magazine.)

[6]

Sheriff Jim: Living Legend of the Law

The Flournoy name is an old and honorable one. The family came to America as Swiss immigrants more than 350 years ago. Originally of French descent, the family had fled to Switzerland after the Massacre of the Protestants on St. Bartholomew's Day, August 24, 1572. Almost one hundred years later Jacob Flournoy and his nephew, Jean Jacques Flournoy, joined the first settlers in the state of Virginia. All the Flournoys in the United States today are descendants of these two men.

Just as some families produce more than their fair share of preachers, doctors, or army officers, the Flournoy specialty was lawmen. There were Flournoys wearing a badge when they first came to Texas with Moses Austin's colony and there have continued to be lawmen in the family since the days of the Texas Republic.

Tom Flournoy was a deputy sheriff in Colorado County, Texas at the turn of the century in 1900. Tom fathered six boys, and three of them became Texas lawmen. Royce was a Texas Ranger prior to his death in 1957. Mike had been Sheriff of Wharton County, Texas, since 1952; he had been hired as a deputy in that county when he was only eighteen. That was not really old enough, but the sheriff doing the hiring had not bothered to ask him his age. He was a Flournoy and that was all that mattered. Flournoys made good lawmen. Mike worked for the legendary Sheriff "Buckshot" Lane until Lane resigned to run for a Congressional seat. Mike was then until his death in 1978, Sheriff, following in the path already laid out for him by his older brother, Jim.

T. J. (Jim) Flournoy was born in 1900. He grew up with a horse and a gun and was an expert with both. Compared to his brother, Mike, Jim was a late starter; he did not become a deputy sheriff until the age of twenty. Being a deputy in sparsely populated Kenedy County was no full-time job however, and young Jim doubled as "top hand" on the McGill Ranch in South Texas.

Old man McGill had a quirk that was more irritating to the lean and lanky cowhand than a burr under a saddle blanket. Every time Flournoy broke and trained a cutting horse for his range "string," the old man would sell the animal at the first opportunity that presented itself. Their confrontation was inevitable. "You sell another cutting horse out from under me, and I'm gonna quit!"

McGill did and Flournoy did what he had promised to do, telling the old man before he left, "They're your horses and I know you're in the business to sell cattle and horses, but I gotta back my words. I hate to turn in my badge but I figger I can always get a job in Harris County, so I'm heading for Houston."

Jim packed his saddle and boarded the train. When it stopped for repairs near the state prison farm between Richmond and Sugarland, a group of "high riders" (mounted prison guards) were working some convicts along the railroad right-of-way.

"Need another hand?" Flournoy asked a bored-looking guard on a bay horse. The question was meant to be a joke, but the guard was not smiling. As captain, he was considering the question seriously as he inspected lean and brawny six-foot-four-inch Flournoy with a critical eye.

"Got a gun?" the captain asked.

"Of course I've got a gun," Flournoy said as he jerked a thumb over his shoulder toward the railroad coach behind him. "Got a rifle, a saddle, and a pistol in my bedroll."

"Get 'em and get back on up here. You're hired," drawled the Captain.

Jim Flournoy has been a lawmen ever since—Deputy Sheriff of Colorado County, state cattle inspector, Deputy Sheriff of Fayette County, Texas Ranger, and, since 1946, Sheriff of Fayette County. He has been a lawman for more than half a century, he figures.

Jim Flournoy has outlived the allotted four score and ten, but the decades have left as little clue to their passage as the outlaws who have tried to bring down the tall, stalwart man. Flournoy is still a trim man with a clear gaze; the hand that shakes uncontrollably when holding a cup of coffee steadies with the weight of a gun, and the marksmanship that made him a legend in his own time is still on target. He patrols Fayette County in a new air-conditioned Oldsmobile, which is a long way removed from the horseback patrols that he once made along the Rio Grande in the "Big Bend" country of West Texas. The horse has been replaced by a piece of Detroit machinery and the bandidos, murderers, and bank robbers have been replaced by burglars, petty thieves, and a few college kids who come home on the weekends "and drag their damned dope and dirty books back to this here town."

The spirit and humor that make his tales of nostalgia sparkle are sadly lacking when he recounts current escapades in his low, monotonous rumble of a voice. "Ninety percent of the crime that's committed around here is done by outsiders. Those fancy rich folks from out of Houston wanna come up here on the weekends and be gentlemen farmers, well, they're just sittin' ducks for burglars the rest of the week."

Few prisoners in the antiquated stone jail spend more than a week as guests of the county and the charge usually is hot checks. The sheriff's biggest case in recent months was finding some hog thieves. The culprits had cut a fence and butchered the loot on the spot, leaving only some tire tracks and hog entrails as evidence for the sheriff and his deputies to study. A brief investigation convinced the sheriff that it would be needless to rush for the arrest of the suspects, and the sheriff did not like to hurry himself or his "boys." The Chief Deputy was the same age as Sheriff Jim, and his other deputy, a scarlet-faced man about fifty years his junior, was so grossly obese any quick move into action would have been impossible even when he was not wedged into a heavy, old wooden arm chair, which he usually was.

But the sheriff did not have to hurry. The hogs were diseased. The plan for apprehending the thieves was to "sit back and wait." A daily check on admittances to local hospitals would eventually yield up some very sick hog rustlers.

With such a decline in the caliber of his antagonists it is not surprising that the sheriff is fond of reminiscing, and when he does so, he prefers the whimsical, the droll, and the capricious rather than the serious tales old lawmen tell with exaggerated solemnity and self-aggrandizement.

"Once run with a Ranger named Pete Crawford," Flournoy says as a sleepy grin spreads across his weathered face. "Fella came runnin' in one day and told old Pete to get on over to Marfa, man over there was fixin' to kill hisself."

"Well, Pete got a move on, goin' jist as fast as he could, but just when he hit this fella's yard he heard a shot. He run on in the house and there was this man running circles around the room, a pistol in his hand, and screamin' with pain. What happened was, the man had missed his head but powder burned his face somethin' awful.

"Ole Pete started chasin' the man around the room and caught him in a turn, took his gun away from him and pushed him into a chair. 'What you think you're a doin?' Pete asked.

" 'You damned fool! Can't you see I'm trying to kill myself?' the feller answered.

"Pete started shaking the bullets out of the gun and asked, 'Why didn't you shoot agin? You still had five shots left.

" 'I would have,' the old boy replied, 'but I couldn't get another standin' shot.' "

Flournoy resigned from the Rangers in 1946 to run for Sheriff of Fayette County. It was an odd campaign because Flournoy's opponent was Jonah Prilop, an old friend and fellow deputy. The two had nothing but praise for each other. Jim won and made Jonah his chief deputy, a post that he still fills.

Changes have been slow in coming to the sheriff's office in La Grange. Jim and Jonah still operate out of the tiny antiquated offices in the courthouse where they started more than thirty years ago and a look around is convincing proof that some of the dust is still in the same place. If the large bulletin board were stripped of its wanted posters and newspaper clippings, there would remain a wealth of nostalgic gems to be uncovered somewhere near the bottom. Clyde Barrow, Raymond Hamilton, and Bonnie Parker helped write a bloody chapter in Texas's criminal history. Jim Flournoy brought Hamilton back to La Grange on a charge of bank robbery. Flournoy does not like gunfighter tales but the dimpled scars of buckshot and bullets that pockmark his body are mute testimony of some smoky episodes.

Whenever veteran lawmen gather to reminisce and swap tales, an exploit of Jim Flournoy's is usually included. An estimated 4,000 to 5,000 thieves, killers, bootleggers, and other assorted criminals have been able to call Huntsville State Prison home because of the efforts of Jim Flournoy to see them housed there. The State Prison was created in 1859 and the first prisoner confined was from Fayette County. Flournoy drawls, "Contrary to certain remarks, I did not deliver that man to the warden."

Some of the respect for the man and his office has to derive from Jim's appearance. He is a slow-walking, slow-talking, sinewy man who, at six-feet-four-inches, towers above almost everyone else, especially after he completes the costume with high-heeled western boots and a white high-crowned Stetson. White shirt, string tie and a single-action Colt .45 with ivory grips round out the wardrobe for the "Best-Dressed Sheriff of 1880." Gary Cooper in *High Noon* is the closest facsimile that can be drawn for anyone born in this century. He has been the stereotype in hundreds of dime-store novels, but when Jim Flournoy passes on to his just rewards his type of lawmen will be as extinct as the dodo bird.

When the new sheriff took office in 1946 at the age of forty-six, he was well-equipped with a wide knowledge of law enforcement and a broad sense of humor, two assets that have kept him in office ever since and have made him a "Living Legend of the Law," as he has been referred to by the *Houston Chronicle,* among others. He was no stranger to Fayette County or the Chicken Ranch. The sheriff and Miss Jessie each recognized and respected the other's professional expertise.

The new sheriff did not sweep into office like a new broom, but he did make an immediate improvement in the communications system between his office and the county's most popular business establishment. Installation of a direct telephone line between the Ranch and the sheriff's office in the old stone courthouse eliminated the nightly trips that had been a part of Sheriff Loessin's evening ritual. Jim made a call each night at ten o'clock to pick up on the gossip of the day, and, occasionally, Miss Jessie would call him to have an obnoxious customer removed. Because of her confinement to a wheelchair, Miss Jessie could no longer act as both madam and bouncer. The old iron rod she had used to enforce discipline in earlier days was too much for her arthritic hands; the phone beside her wheelchair was its replacement.

A whorehouse is not the type of business in which the customers prefer to pay by check or credit card. Furthermore, the Chicken Ranch had a strict policy against accepting checks, the exception being state payroll checks. At the end of a busy day the cash on hand made quite a bundle, a fact that had not escaped the attention of a couple of self-employed bandits from Houston. And it all looked so easy. Here was an isolated farmhouse with a madam confined to a wheelchair, customers who would rather be robbed than become dead heroes, and protected by a hick sheriff.

The robbers followed standard operating procedures for this type of job. The customers and girls alike were ordered to stand against a wall, were selected one at a time to be stripped of anything of value, and then were tied and told to lie face down on the floor. Since Miss Jessie's small, twisted body was already a prisoner of the wheelchair, the thieves did not bother tying her up; she quite obviously was not going anywhere. They did demand her money and she handed it to them. But the greedy little rascals wanted more, and she told them where to find it.

Miss Jessie sent them to search through a very deep and rather messy closet. They did find money and they wanted more! They searched through ancient hat boxes, inside old shoes, the linings of coats, and between stacks of linens. Escaping feathers from shredded pillows filled the air as emptied cartons, old quilts, and vintage magazines came hurtling toward the open door to dam its entrance.

And while the overly busy beavers were so preoccupied, Miss Jessie picked up the phone beside her chair and said, "I'm being robbed." The thieves were still ransacking the closet when Sheriff Jim walked in and arrested them all with ease.

The thieves had their day in court, but it was perhaps a greater ordeal for Miss Jessie than it was for the defendants. Miss Jessie had to be carried up the steps of the courthouse for her appearance at the trial.

Both of the would-be robbers were paroled, but one of them was also wanted by the state of Oklahoma on a hijacking charge. He was arrested in Houston, made bond, and was killed in Beaumont his first week out. The other would-be robber violated his parole, which was then revoked. He was sent to prison and died a short time later.

It was also only a short time later that Miss Jessie turned over the management of her business to a newcomer at the Ranch, although she continued to reign from her four-poster bed as if it were a throne in the queen's bedchamber. Her health deteriorated rapidly during the fifties. The black woman who had been her maid and companion for more than forty years dressed, fed, bathed, and comforted the ailing madam during her last years at the Chicken Ranch. But these were not Miss Jessie's final years. She spent those last years in San Antonio with her old friend and ex-employee—the wealthy, widowed, and socially prominent "sister."

[7]

Edna Milton's Money: Fantastic Fifties-Super Sixties

Edna Milton's early biography reads like a saga of the Depression. Born to a dirt-poor Oklahoma farm couple, Edna and her sisters (one now a policewoman in Los Angeles) picked cotton like any other Okie lucky enough to have a crop during the dust-bowl years. But Edna found time to sow some wild oats when she was not picking cotton. At sixteen she was pregnant. Her family turned against her with proverbial "don't darken my door" rhetoric and Edna left the furrowed Oklahoma farm for the seamy side of Oklahoma City. The baby died.

Edna moved through the ranks of her profession. She also moved to Austin, Texas, bought a home, and took a husband. She moved again in 1952 to La Grange and the Chicken Ranch. She was twenty-three years old, an attractive young woman with auburn hair and a slim figure well-suited to the styles of the era, which included waist-cinchers, toreador pants, sling pumps, and perma-lift bras. Edna also had a sharp wit, a sense of humor, and a facile mind. She became as shrewd a businesswoman as her mentor.

The fifties have been described as the decade nostalgically remembered for absolutely nothing. But that is not how they are remembered in La Grange; the fifties were its zenith, its heyday, and its epitome of importance. Fame and fortune for the dreary little town was the fallout from its most visited tourist attraction. The second most visited business was the old filling station on the corner where initiates stopped to ask directions, drink an R.C., and munch on a moon pie while building up a new batch of courage.

The Aggies came in pickup trucks, Houston punks in hot rods, U.T. students in sedans, and the airmen from Bergstrom came in Air Force helicopters. The shuttle system from "Base" to "House" was better organized than some Urban Transit Systems. When the pilot left Bergstrom A.F.B., fifty miles west of La Grange, he would radio a message to the small airfield in La Grange alerting them to the time of his arrival and number of passengers. The airport employee taking the message would in turn phone across the street to the manager of the Cottonwood Cafe. The manager of the cafe was also a rancher who owned a nice-sized cattle truck. In La Grange there were no limousines, no buses, and no passenger complaints about the cattle truck.

Rancher/Restauranteur Bob would haul his passengers the two miles to the Ranch and drink beer in the kitchen with Edna or the black attendants until the visiting airmen had completed their business transactions and were ready to be hauled back to the airfield. Sixteen was the usual number of passengers on each trip, and sometimes the ferry ran all night.

Students, farmers, servicemen, and the perennial salesmen put the Chicken Ranch on the national map during the fifties. The house operated at maximum capacity (sixteen girls) and business was so good, especially on weekends, that the line of customers waiting in front of the cement stoop would wind halfway round the big white house.

The Korean War, like wars before, was good for the brothel business. The Army and Air Force bases—there must have been a dozen within a hundred mile radius of La Grange—were staffed to capacity with new draftees. Many became Edna's customers, and a special few became close friends. One young soldier bound for combat asked Edna to keep his dog while he was away. Of course, she did, but he never returned. Many years later the dog was still at the Chicken Ranch and Edna was still melancholy when she thought about the abandoned pet. She felt certain that the dog's owner had been killed.

It is standard operating procedure for houses of prostitution to have a monetary alliance with politicians and law-enforcement agents, but there has never been a shred of evidence, and surprisingly few rumors, indicating that Edna ever had a "deal" going with any one (an alliance, yes, but not a monetary alliance). Edna kept every dime of profit, and a substantial profit it was, with revenues in the millions.

Her success did not go unnoticed. The fifties had indeed been fabulous. The sixties would be farcical. In 1961 Miss Jessie died at the age of 80. Edna Milton, who had been the actual manager of the house for some years, made arrangements with Faye Stewart's heirs to buy the property. Miss Jessie would have liked that.

Edna bought the house, furnishings and slightly more than ten acres of land for $30,000. She made a down payment of $1500 and paid the rest in installments of $200 per month at six percent interest. According to records in the Fayette County Tax Assessor's Office, the price Edna paid was far in excess of the actual market value of the land and the improvements that were probably worth about $8,000 in 1961. It was the Goodwill that came high. But Edna had been in residence for several years. She knew exactly what she was paying for.

Edna was thirty-two years old when she went into business for herself. She was still a pretty woman, if perhaps a bit dumpy. She liked hats and usually wore one when shopping in La Grange. But she was no longer fashionable, her clothes were dated, and she refused adamantly to shorten her skirts when that became the trend. The bright-red hair had turned dull and was going gray, but her eyes still remained as piercing as a laser. In appearance, she could have passed for any middle-class, middle-aged housewife of the community.

The similarity ended with appearances. Although Edna was a shrewd and foxy businesswoman, with the demeanor of a Marine drill sargeant, she was also romantic and sentimental. Installed in Miss Jessie's former bedroom, complete with Miss Jessie's four-poster bed, Edna devoted her leisure time to reading and writing poetry, which represented quite a contrast to the movie magazines, the rags such as *True Confessions*, and the cheap paperbacks that were favored by her employees.

Philosophy, history, and theology were favorite subjects to which Edna applied enough life experience to draw common-sense conclusions. Her friends would gather around the kitchen table for serious conversation and heated arguments on a wide range of topics. Although she lacked a formal education, Edna could hold her own in a group of intellectuals. When intelligence failed, wit saw her through.

Edna's friends and lovers were not customers. Friends visited only the kitchen, never the bedroom, even though all of them were men. She chose her lovers with discretion. Very few men were allowed the privilege of sharing her big four-poster bed or the intimacy of her ultra-feminine bedroom that held a hodgepodge of gilt and crystal trinkets, floral prints, lace trims, and velvet coverings. Fewer still felt comfortable in those surroundings.

She married her second husband, Johnny Luke, shortly after buying the Chicken Ranch. Johnny shared her bedroom for several years, but they were ultimately divorced. When they separated he took all of the couple's assets except for Edna's business and a heavily mortgaged rented house in Austin.

Edna's pets were more devoted. Her favorite was a small, squatty white terrier that had the run of the house and was spoiled and pampered by the girls who lived there. They took Trixie into their beds, gave her baths and manicures, and slipped her delicacies from the dining table, which is why she was so squatty. And the customers loved her.

"Show 'em, Trixie, show 'em how our girls make their money," the black maid would call, and the little terrier would roll over on her back, squirming and shaking, little red toenails beating the air in a staccato rhythm.

Edna loved Trixie as well as all animals. There were usually several dogs of nondescript lineage living at the Chicken Ranch. A couple of them would greet the visitors with a wagging tail and a cold nose, but behind the tall wooden fence there was another dog or two whose disposition was not as friendly. Their barking always announced new arrivals in the compound and discouraged the local teenagers, who were too young and broke to be customers, from pranks and mischief. The dogs would dissuade aspiring "peeping toms" in their endeavors, but these customers of the future would merely be disgruntled and upset with the animals. There was no lingering malice toward Edna but there would have been if she had called the sheriff or a bouncer to rout out the rascals.

[8]

A Working Girl: Past, Present, and Plans for Tomorrow

When Edna signed the mortgage the Chicken Ranch looked like a typical Texas farmhouse, having whitewashed pine siding, dark green trim, and no recognizable architectual style. The rooms, which had been added haphazardly as the need arose, numbered fourteen eventually and led from one room to another in an absurd maze. There was no red velvet, nor were there gilt-framed nudes, uniformed maids, or chandeliers. There was not even a piano player. There was a juke box and a Coke machine. The rest of the furnishings were a hodgepodge of basic necessities—a bed, a bureau, a sink. It could not have survived in a red-light district; it did not have the class.

Edna's first move after buying the house was to add on another room, a dining room, which was the last addition ever made to the house. She also installed air-conditioning units in the bedrooms. This was not done to attract more trade but, rather, represented "employee benefits." Imagine these poor working girls on a humid day or night! It is sweaty work!

Except for these two improvements, the house and furnishings remained almost the same for the last twenty years that it operated as a whorehouse. The high fence that surrounded the house changed color from green to white in recent years, but the two cement steps at the entrance felt the step of several generations of men who were scrutinized closely through the heavily screened door, the attendant on the other side aided by a brilliant floodlight that clearly illuminated the unpretentious entry.

Miss Edna's staff of working girls was in a constant state of flux. A new girl in a brothel is like a new entreé on a menu, bringing back old customers to sample new fare. But Edna's attendants were more permanent. They were paid well to encourage loyalty and reliability. A good attendant, who usually doubled as maid, and sometimes as cook, knew the clients well. She knew when to unlock the screened door and when to turn a customer away. Although she was invariably black, she did not admit visitors who were black or Mexican. "Sorry honey, I can't let ya'll come in. Them's Miss Edna's rules," she'd say as she closed the heavy wooden door.

A white customer who was admitted had to look presentable, could not be visibly drunk, and was not allowed to do any loud cussin' or talking dirty. Once a customer had passed the visual scrutiny and verbal interrogation, he was politely asked to take a seat in the parlor. The warm-toned floral carpet and Victorian woodwork in the room gave evidence to its age. The woodwork was old, in fact, while the carpet only appeared that way, like some remnant of Aunt Tillie's big remodeling spree of 1910. Two wooden benches and some mismatched chairs, probably the same ones Miss Jessie bought during her improvement program during the twenties, sat against opposite walls. The customers were seated on one side and Miss Edna's girls on the other, just like a high school prom. Every third chair had an ashtray on a stand at its side. Mirrors on two walls did little to alleviate the gloomy atmosphere. Curtains and exterior-louvered shutters were always kept closed tightly to assure privacy from peeping toms. Only the juke box and cigarette machine kept the whole place in perspective. Without this touch of commercialism the whole place would have resembled a parsonage in a terribly poor parish.

For a quarter visitors could listen to a country-western record guaranteed not to be less than five years old, and seventy-five cents bought a pack of cigarettes. This was during the days of ten-cent songs and thirty-five-cent cigarettes so anyone paying seventy-five cents must have been nervous. Either it was his first time out, or he was scared of catching a dose, or afraid he might meet someone he knew before he could settle his business and get out. Edna sold quite a few cigarettes.

In a wide hallway leading to the bedrooms was a large cooler stocked with Cokes. It appeared that only the Coca-Cola Bottling Company made deliveries. The Cokes cost one dollar. The girls always asked for one and, of course, the customer was supposed to buy one for himself too. The only real bargain the Chicken Ranch ever had was sex. All other goods were overpriced to discourage loitering.

The fourteen-room house was a long way from elegant decadence; shabby comes close. There was a master bedroom for the madam in residence, the Queen's bedchamber, you might say. There was a large old-fashioned kitchen, the favorite gathering place for friends who were there to visit rather than to do business. But you had to be a *real* good friend to gain access to the kitchen, whereas the bedrooms were open to almost anyone with the fare (excluding blacks and chicanos, of course!). There was also a large dining room where the girls took their two meals a day. The cook, like all other domestic help, was a local black woman and it was soul food all the way! There is more going for a country whorehouse than not being hassled by the cops; the food is delicious.

The working girls' bedrooms were both a home and place of business. The rooms were comfortable but the furnishings drab. Cheap, imitation Early American was the prevailing theme for nightstands, beds, and dressers. Washable chenille bedspreads came in a variety of colors; magenta, red, gold, and turquoise. Each bedroom had its own tiny lavatory cubicle equipped with an ultra-small sink. The house also had six bathrooms.

That did not leave sixteen bedrooms, and sometimes there were sixteen girls in residence at one time so there was some doubling up. Yes, Virginia, there really were lesbians, or more accurately, bisexuals, even in a wholesome country whorehouse like the Chicken Ranch. None of the ex-employees ever is one herself, but she always roomed just down the hall from two who were.

At the time of Marvin's Massacre the going rate for fifteen minutes of plain old screwin' was $15.00, or $1.00 a minute. Since each girl usually had between five and twenty dates a day, the average would be about twelve. If you put that in your calculator and compute, it adds up to over $500,000 a year in gross income. And that is not counting the take on the Coke and cigarette machines, which in itself was enough to cover Edna's charitable donations to a worthy cause. Her number one cause was the continual operation of her whorehouse.

When a prostitute lives in a house it is customary for her to turn seventy-five percent of her earnings over to the madam. While no exact figures on the Chicken Ranch have been divulged, it would be reasonable to assume that this standard rate applied. If this seems like an exhorbitant cut for the house, compute again and you will find the average girl clearing over $300.00 per week. She had no expenses! Her employer provided food, rent, laundry, and even the weekly visit to the doctor. She had no worries about utilities or transportation, but only the taxes on the income she was willing to declare, which the IRS never questioned, but which undoubtedly left a lot of leeway for plenty of loopholes.

The madam did have expenses but in a country whorehouse they are not on the grand scale that her sisters in the city have to contend with. There are no bribes to cops, judges, nor any district attorneys. There are no city taxes, city utilities, nor any advantage at all to moving to a high-rent district to attract a better clientele. In the country you are number one and you do not have to try harder. Unlike Ma Bell, when you are the only whorehouse in town you can damn sure act like it.

Edna paid the taxes, insurance, utilities, food bills, doctor, two attendants, maids, cook, and laundry bills. There was a small mountain of towels after a busy day, but sheets were changed only once a week. Edna did not believe in being frivolous.

City madams are also accustomed to dressing their stable well. The girls who worked at the house of Hattie Valdez in Austin had charge accounts at the finest stores in town, and the now-extinct Parisian Peytons was one of their favorite stores. It closed at about the same time Hattie was forced into retirement. Edna's girls bought their own clothes, usually in La Grange. A typical afternoon costume was a well-fitting pant suit, just like the ones worn by the mommies going to PTA. But mommies rarely wear gold slippers. The girls at Edna's adored gold slippers. Any time of day or night, they wore their gold slippers like a badge. Evening work clothes were a bit more dressy—robes, gowns, and evening pajamas were worn in a multitude of prints and colors. Their clothes were glittery, gauche, and, at Miss Edna's, cheap.

It is quite obvious that a prostitute on her own could make a lot more money but, she would have to hustle her own business, which is against the law. She could go to jail and get a record in addition to a fine. This prospect alone makes the seventy-five percent collected by the madam seem cheap enough. She had security in an old, established house like the one in La Grange. She knew that she would not be busted. This was an important reason for all the girls, but especially for those who were in hiding from abusive or abandoned husbands, cast-off pimps and, quite often, parents and family. They could not afford the publicity or the record.

At least half of the girls in the profession have had one or more children. Ironically enough, pregnancy is not an occupational hazard. Even without precautions, the busy prostitute rarely gets pregnant, a fact that the medical profession has studied with amused curiosity. Doctors have theorized that extensive sexual activity causes fatigue of the sphincter muscles, which in turn causes a malfunction of the Kristeller plug, a mucous plug at the mouth of the uterus descending into the vagina. During orgasm a contraction of these muscles causes the plug to descend into the vagina and act as a ladder for the sperm climbing to meet the ovum. These biological facts support the old saying, "God protects the working girl."

But prostitutes are not impressed with theories. Contraception information is a favorite subject of conversation, right up there with "movie stars," "beauty secrets," "true love," and "celebrities I have _____" (supply your own word, anything will fit). Many girls believe contraception is unnecessary, not because of Kristeller's plug, but because they believe that different strains of semen destroy each other. Those who do not share in this primitive belief take birth control pills, not only for their contraceptive benefits but also, if taken every day of the month, some types halt menstruation and enable her to work every day.

Many girls use an antiseptic douche after each client, another reason the house has an advantage over hustling if a douche is her bag. The recipes for the mix are as fanciful and imaginative as an old whore's dreams.

Condoms never are offered to a customer. To do so might cause him to suspect venereal disease. If he requests one, however, it will be given to him, free of charge. Do not assume this request for a condom is because he is concerned about her becoming pregnant. Whether free or paid for, the prevailing male attitude is "she can take care of herself."

When a prostitute does become pregnant, the statistics show an extraordinary number of spontaneous abortions for members of her profession. Whether this can be attributed to a change in the genital organs or wishful thinking has not been clearly determined. Dr. Norman Vincent Peale's *Power of Positive Thinking* should at any rate, be read by all ambitious whores wanting to increase profits and cut down on sick leave.

If spontaneity does not come through there is always good old "Doctor Quack." Every town has one; larger towns have two or three. He had a rather lucrative business before abortions became legal. There were also a lot of self-induced abortions prior to the new law, but abortion was much more common among the amateurs than it was among professional girls.

Approximately half of all prostitutes have had at least one child and some have had several. And, like mothers in all walks of life, some are good parents, and some are rotten ones. More than half of the girls at the ranch furnished sole support for their minor children. Many had been married, usually at a very early age, and had been abandoned later by their husbands. They were left with small children to care for but had no marketable assets or salable skills. The children were boarded usually with the girl's family, who was unaware that the money that they were receiving from the mother was the wages of sin. If the family had its suspicions about the large sums of money that an uneducated girl was capable of earning, these doubts were rarely expressed.

[9]

The Sheriff and the Madam: The Famous and the Infamous

Once Edna had the deed to the Chicken Ranch locked away in her safety deposit box, she added to the repertoire of her performers. The missionary position was really getting to be a bore, even for the rednecks and Baptists in the boonies. That is not to say that Edna was exotic, erotic, or about to get that way. She added the bare minimum in sexual frills needed to keep the boys from Aggieland coming back.

Sexual mores were changing in the sixties. The "girl next door" was willing to give away the simple service Edna had been selling for so many years. But, oral sex was still considered a deviate practice not readily available to young students grabbing "freebies," and group sex was a pastime attributed only to decadent Yankee suburbanites. Adding these two modern "services" to the business cost Edna nothing. Of course, she made a bundle.

During the fifties, and on into the sixties, there was a Thursday-night special for $8.00. For $8.00 of good beer money, the customer had about fifteen minutes of conventional, dull sex. This was certainly never the erotic stuff from which adolescent dreams are made. However, it pays to advertise, and a bureau drawer left slightly open to expose an interesting assortment of erotic paraphenalia could tempt even the two-stroke man to go for the $40 package.

Edna's house usually had between twelve and sixteen girls, and the money was rolling in. She wisely decided to become the town's number one philanthropist, ingratiating herself to the community and building up a solid bloc of good character references. She, like

Jessie, always paid her taxes, and the IRS never took any interest in her or her employees. Edna contributed $10,000 toward the building of a new hospital and $1,000 for the new community swimming pool. Through her support the Little League team was well-equipped with bats, balls, and gloves, a fact that lead sports reporters to refer to the La Grange team as the "La Grange Chicks." The folks in Fayette County were not amused.

When Hurricane Carla hit the Texas Coast, refugees from the storm poured into La Grange from Houston, Galveston, and other Gulf Coast cities. Hundreds were provided shelter at the Fair Grounds, the courthouse, City Hall, and the American Legion hall. But they would not have been provided with a comfortable place to sleep without Johnny Luke. Edna's husband owned a second-hand furniture store in Austin, and he trucked his entire inventory of mattresses to La Grange to help make the unexpected guests a bit more comfortable.

Edna's girls always spent their earnings in La Grange, according to Sheriff Jim, but another merchant was not quite as impressed with their buying power. Said he, "They only had a payroll of a dozen or so out there. How much money you figure twelve whores gonna spend?" Local bankers agreed. They didn't really spend all that much. They saved a lot.

If Sheriff Jim was enamored with the house when he first became Sheriff, there is evidence to suggest that he became even more infatuated down through the years. "It's a clean place to go to," Flournoy reasoned. "Ain't got no pimps, no narcotics, no alcohol, and no trouble.

"I've been Sheriff all these years and there's nevrah been no rapes. And we ain't got a bunch of pregnant gals in the school. It just don't have no ill effects . . . lots of respectable businessmen take their sons out there when they git old enough. I ain't nevrah got no complaints 'cept one time when some crackpot son-of-a-bitch called me up at two o'clock in the morning."

Houston newsman, Larry Connors, put it so aptly, "He makes that whorehouse sound like a damn county non-profit recreational facility."

It has been suggested by some that the Chicken Ranch was connected to organized crime. If this were the case, Jim Flournoy would have lived better than he did on his salary as sheriff. He lives in a modest, brick home on the west side of La Grange with his wife, Gladys. They have no children. Folks in La Grange could set a watch by his noon ritual of going home to have lunch with his wife, a habit as regular as his phone calls to the Ranch. The Ranch has been in the sights of some of the lower echelon of the crime world, but not because they wanted a piece of the business. Burglary and armed robbery, short-term gains, were more their style.

An Austin artist who grew up in La Grange reminisced, "Any trouble at the Chicken Ranch and Jim would go out and womp the guy on the head with a pistol butt, no trouble, no publicity. If there was a knifing or shootin' over in colored town he'd go to the scene—but if the culprit was gone, Jim didn't look for him. He went back to his office and waited. The guy would turn himself in in the morning. Everybody always did. Had too much respect for him to do otherwise."

It also has been suggested that the sheriff had an interest in the business and actually ran the ranch. Technically, this is not true; he had no monetary investment in the house. He did, however, control all activities at the house. No girl ever worked there without his approval. He knew who the customers were; some were barred at his request. If the house was visited by prominent dignitaries, politicians, or celebrities, he set up the appointments. The sheriff was kept informed of every move and every action through communications via the "hot line."

New girls at the Ranch were routinely "mugged" and finger-printed by the sheriff before they were accepted as employees. If they had a criminal background, they were not allowed to stay. Edna would not violate the Mann Act and hire a girl who came from outside the state of Texas, nor accept any girl who had a pimp. The girl's personal male friends were not allowed to visit the Ranch and if they did so, the girl was told to leave.

The sheriff's routine investigation of every new girl was done primarily to protect the business and Edna Milton, but numerous girls were identified and held on outstanding warrants from other law enforcement agencies throughout the United States. The F.B.I. frequently came by the Ranch to leave pictures of "Wanted" women with Edna.

The girls who were allowed to work at the Chicken Ranch

surpassed the average worker in loyalty and devotion to their employer. Some stayed for many years, and during the last several years of operation the turnover in employees was almost nil.

In 1962 the State Attorney General, Will Wilson, in his bid for a seat in the Senate, went on a moral crusade to rid Texas of hustlers, whores, pimps, and gamblers. Mr. Wilson had a stack of complaints ready to be served on these entrepreneurs, including one against Edna Milton, but neither the district attorney nor the county attorney in Fayette County would take the complaint.

Mr. Wilson's crusade changed Galveston from a sophisticated, chic resort into a gaudy, dirty playpen for adolescents—and Texans still have not forgiven him. He made waves while trying for a landslide and his bid for the Senate failed. The woods had not been as full of morally indignant voters as he needed to get elected.

Although no formal complaint had been filed against her, Edna chose to "pull in her head" during Mr. Wilson's crusade, a crusade that Sheriff Jim Flournoy called "a damned publicity stunt."

While discreetly letting regular customers in through a back door, Edna went through the pretense of shutting the house down until the election was over. After Wilson's defeat he took a job in Washington from which he was subsequently fired.

There were other times when Edna had to "cool it" for a while. Crusaders always singled out the Chicken Ranch as the target of their salvation because its name was easily recognized, and it made good copy for the press. But with Edna's maintaining the lowest of profiles, and the crusaders receiving no cooperation at all from any branch of law enforcement, disgruntled do-gooders went away seeking some other cause. Life at the Chicken Ranch carried on as it had been doing for more than a century. It was business as usual.

[10]

Company's Coming!: Night Work and Daydreams

The waiting room was hot, dreary, and dim. The girls were all rather pretty, at least in the available light. There was any type to choose from—pixie brunettes, a redhead with freckles, two with blonde wigs. They were an assorted group in size, shape, and coloring, but one thing they all had in common, besides the gold shoes, was posture.

They all sat with their legs crossed, foot pumping to some imaginary rhythm (they were all playing the same tune!), shoulders curved round like a shield for their chests, and they all looked like they were sitting on a spring, ready to catapult toward whoever chose them.

Chosen, the girl takes her "date" of the quarter hour by the arm, leads him down a wide hallway, past the Coke box, and into her room.

She says her name is Carrie. "What's your?" They exchange pleasantries, get acquainted. "Where are you from? What do you do? What would you like to do now?"

He finds himself maneuvered into a chair next to the brightest light he has seen since coming into the house. The back of his neck is gently stroked while Carrie gives her sales pitch. The minimum rate is $15.00 but $5.00 more buys a lot more fun. For an additional $10.00 she makes no promises, but tries her best to give a seductive leer that does not quite come off. Carrie is a good salesperson; she stops her pitch at what she believes is his "ready cash" limit. Embarrassing a customer would be bad manners and bad business relations.

The price agreed on, Carrie leaves her date to undress while she carries the money to an attendant. The slat-bottom chair is cold, goosebumps cover his legs. He shivers and feels ill-at-ease. He wonders if he will be able to get an erection in this cold, uncomfortable room. And he worries about the humiliation if he cannot. Carrie returns and he watches an obviously patent, but nonetheless stimulating, undressing routine. His worries about virility disappear.

Again she maneuvers him onto the cold, slatted chair, then inspects his genitals, a standard practice at any good house, and an unbroken rule at the Chicken Ranch. Satisfied with appearances, Carrie leads her customer to the small corner sink where his genitals are lathered and rinsed in a flow of warm water. He is thinking about the time that has already elapsed . . . perhaps eight or ten minutes already gone out of an expensive fifteen.

But the time left is time enough.

She gives him a smile and a kiss to make him believe he has pleased her. "You're nice," she says as she slides away from him, thinking he really *was* nice, and she hopes he comes back again. He had been gentle, clean, and undemanding, probably because he was still a young man of no more than twenty-two or so. Older men were often crude and boorish, or sometimes cruel. They were never shy or embarrassed for themselves, but often tried to humiliate her. Some men would not talk to her at all, as if she were not another human being capable of communicating, but a gadget, a gimmick to serve his needs, or a machine to be rented by the quarter-hour. They always left her with a lingering feeling of degradation that was hard to shake.

Carrie bathes herself, dresses, and repairs her hair and makeup before escorting her date to the front door. She asks him to please come back again, as she knows he will. He was "their" kind of customer.

It is not a busy night. Carrie returns to the back room that serves as a lounge when not needed as an extra bedroom and waits for the bell that rings whenever the attendant unlatches the screen for a new arrival.

Carrie was one of several working mothers at the Ranch. When complimented on her name she laughs, "Oh, it's really Clara, but that sounds so country. I had a real exotic name when I first came to work here, but I don't want to be called that anymore."

She has a son of thirteen. She gives her own age as thirty. Long brown hair is Carrie's only striking feature; when complimented on it she looks self-conscious, then confides she is wearing a wig. Showgirl eyelashes need no explanation.

Prostitution may not be synonymous with "The Good Life," but, as Carrie explained, "I really like it at the ranch, but I can't stay here forever. Like, I mean, my kid is getting older, he's goin' to start finding things out. Kids are smart!" She smiles, enjoying a private moment of maternal pride.

"I don't want him to know I work here. What I'd really like to do now is leave here and then get married. You can't get a husband working in a whorehouse. The kid lives with my folks. Daddy has a little acreage over close to Tyler. It's a good place for kids. No running with rough kids like in the city. I grew up there and if things had gone different I guess I'd still be back there.

"I wasn't no wild kid in high school . . . lots of 'em were worse than me! I liked this one boy an awful lot, knowed him all my life, never went with no other boy. We started messin' around in about the sixth or seventh grade and I got pregnant when I was sixteen . . . Gawd, was I scared! So was Elwood, he figgered my Daddy wuz gonna kill him! We finally told Elwood's Mama about what we'd done and she told my Mama and next thing I knew we wuz married. Don't recall anybody asking me what I *wanted* to do—guess it was too late for that," she says with a smile.

"Elwood didn't know nothin' and me neither. At least I didn't just run off without seeing to my kid like he done his. He run off before the little one was even born! And I ain't seen him since. Ain't seen his folks neither. They moved off too, not caring no more about his kid than he did. I ain't tried to find him—don't wanna find him. My folks love my boy and take good care of him. I send money and get to spend a few days a month with him. It's alright.

"I didn't go into this life right after Elwood run off. First thing I done wuz have that baby. There weren't any jobs in Tyler that paid anything. Besides, I didn't know anything.

"I had this best friend since seventh grade, Margaret Ann, calls herself Maggie now. She moved to Houston with her folks when we wuz in high school, but we'd kept in touch. So she said come on down to Houston, she could get me a job where she worked. I figgered since she'd always been dummer'n me, if she could earn $25 a day so could I. Easy.

"I went to work in this joint out on Westheimer same as where she worked, only I didn't make any $25 a day like she said. What Margaret Ann hadn't told me wuz, she usually had a trick lined up for after she wuz done waitin' tables. She made as much in a half-hour after work as she did from waitin' tables all night.

"My folks had agreed to keep the baby and I wuz supposed to send 'em some money every week except I never had any. Mama wuz raisin' hell! So sometimes I started doin' the same as Margaret Ann if I really liked the guy, only I wuz scared. I kept thinking about what if I got caught! What would my Daddy say? Hell, and my kid would find out someday maybe, if I had a record with the police. I didn't like it much.

"I'd had a couple of dates with this one guy and got to telling him how I felt, about my kid and all. He told me I oughta be working in a house, but I told him I didn't even know where a house was. He knew though; knew quite a few as a matter of fact. I didn't like that idea any better than hustling like I'd been doin'. In fact, I liked it even less. I mean, man, you get busted workin' in a house and you're just a whore from a whorehouse! Everybody knows exactly what you are! At least with hustling on your own there's more room to make excuses.

"But this guy I'm telling you about convinced me to at least go talk to this woman he knew who had a house in Houston—no harm in that. And I'm glad I did. She was real nice. She told me about Edna Milton's place and it sounded real good to me. She even helped me to get on here, I wuz so dumb.

"I've worked here for quite a while. Made a whole lot of money! I really like the girls here—Edna, and the other help. We're really good friends and I don't know where else I'd want to go. I guess I'm really happy here, at least for now. I've got lots of time left to catch me a husband." She looks wistfully out a window, and you wonder if she really believes what she just said.

The attendant's bell announces a new arrival, and Carrie breaks her reverie. One of Edna's many rules stated clearly, "When the call bell rings that there are guests in the parlor all boarders are expected to go into the parlor immediately."

Edna's literary talent left a lot to be desired, but she knew how to get a point across. Her list of Rules and Regulations (reprinted by permission of Kent Demaret, *The Many Faces of Marvin Zindler*, copyright 1976, The Hunt Company) was required reading for all employees and is reproduced here with grammatical idiosyncrasies intact.

Rules and Regulations

"I, Edna Milton, a femme sole trader own this building and all the furnishings, also 11.32 acres of land duly recorded in the Fayette County Courthouse, La Grange, Texas 78945.

"This place nor I have any connection what so ever with any other place mob or syndicate of any type.

"This place is individually owned by me.

"To whom it may concern to all living on these premises.

"If any one here is an illiterate or of sub normal intelligence they had better have some one read and explain this to them.

"Read this book regularly (about once a month) if you want to live here.

"These rules will be followed by all boarders no exceptions.

"Any one having no intentions of following these rules might just as will leave now.

"Absolutely no narcotics are permitted on these premises if any narcotics are found or suspected the law will be called immediately.

"Drinking is not permitted during visiting hours and any one doing so will be asked or ordered to leave.

"In short dope heads, pill heads and drunks are not permitted to live here regardless of who they are.

"Thieves, liars and ribbers are not needed or wanted here when I ask a boarder a question I demand an honest to the point answer.

"What you do away from here and away from this county is your business as long as it has no reflection on me or my business.

"I don't like cliques in my house and I don't want to walk into any bodys room and see a group of people on the bed, chairs or the floor the shinning room and parlor have a sufficient number of chairs to accommodate every one here for discussions and other get togethers. Beds are not to be wallowed in that is what hogs do. I expect all borders to take care of my furniture even if they don't know how to take care of their own.

"There are nine rooms here and I consider it as hiring short of boarders where there are only eight boarders here. If I had three more rooms and had boarders in every room at all times I wouldn't consider it as having too many boarders for amount of company coming here. There are times when things are slow, but the same holds time with any occupation anywhere in the world. Any occupation has its off season.

"No boarder will have a regular room unless I have told her otherwise also at my discretion there may be two boarders in one room, this comes under my business and I don't care to discuss the reason for so doing so with anyone any time a boarder regardless of who she may be decides to interogate me in any manner she may show proper credentials and a badge authorizing her to do so and then get out.

"I expect all regular boarders to be here at least ¾ of the time otherwise she will considered a transit boarder.

"When a boarder is off I expect a phone call the day before she returns if for some legitimate reason a boarder is not able to return as skeduled I expect a phone call advising me so I can make arrangements if necessary. I don't always appreciate being caught short of boarders due to somebody else's negligence and erresponsibility on the day a boarder returns to work after being off she is expected to be here no later 6p.m. bus skedules excluded and only then if the bus arrives at a reasonable hour.

"When a boarder plans to leave I want to know in advance unless they are leaving permanently as well as when they plan to return anytime a boarder leaves this house without my knowledge or permission she will pack her things. "If a boarder has a pimp that comes under the heading of her business if she does not have a pimp it still comes under the heading of her business not mine or any other boarder living on these premises as long as a boarder takes care of her business does not interfere into my business and the business of other boarders she can live here her business is hers and my business is mine. I consider myself quite capabel of taking care of my own business and I will do just that.

"If a boarder has people she should advise them to keep their nose out of my business. I don't want my business as well as their business in a mix master.

"This is not and never will be a house of (white slavery) as long as I continue to operate this boarding house, no pimp will ever own it if they ever get that idea they do sin as much as they could possibly sin.

"As I said this is not a white slavery place and never will be as long as I have any thing to do with it therefore I will not have a boarder in my house with an excess amount of bruises and a lot of tatoos on their body. Cattle are branded for identification, tatoos are much the same as brands. I can remember my name without them, Can you?

"Boarders are permitted to see their pimp or lover one night a week (never more than that). Boarders may call the [deleted] Inn or the [deleted] Motel for reservation when their lovers come into town.

"A boarders lover may pick her up on week nights at 3:15 a.m. she is to return no later than 3 p.m. except by permission.

"All boarders and pimps are to stay off the back road.

"The phone is to be used by everyone here I don't want any boarder to receive more than one phone call per day and that is from home, three minutes is sufficient time for any one to talk concerning family or their business.

"Anyone caught discussing my business on the phone won't live here money is not to be discussed on the phone any time phone calls are subject to be monitored. Remember don't let your mouth overload your capabilities.

"Phone calls are to be made between the hours of 12:00 noon and 3 a.m. no exceptions.

"The cook comes to work at 11:00 a.m. and breakfast is served shortly there after food is removed from the table by 12:30 p.m.

"Dinner is served at 4 p.m. or shortly there after.

"No one is to skip a meal because they have company and then expect their food later, they can always excuse themselves when dinner is served or make arrangements with the cook to put their dinner away for them. I don't pay the cook to cater to anyone interference with the cook irregardless which boarder they will leave here as soon as I know about it.

"Decent or reasonable manners are expected of everyone eating at my table suitable subjects are to be discussed while eating. Not everyone can eat while filthy talk is going on in fact as far as I am concerned the filthy talk can wait forever.

"No boarder is to leave the dinner table until she has finished eating.

"All boarders dressed and properly made up by 1 p.m. when guests are permitted into the house. Casual dress is appropriate for daytime. Hair should be combed or at least covered with an attractive scarf.

"All boarders are to be dressed in dinner dresses, cocktail dresses or evening pantsuits no later than 7 p.m. Absolutely no casual clothes permitted at night except by special permission.

"The house closes at 3 a.m. so if a boarder expecting an overnight guest they should arrive on week nights about 3:15 a.m. Exeptions by permission only overnight guests on Saturday night should arrive at 3:30 a.m. never earlier.

"When the call bell rings that there are guest in the parlor all boarders are expected to go into the parlor immediately. Exceptions to this rule are only permissable if the boarder is eating dinner, taking a bath, using the commode or else busy entertaining a guest. Long sad faces look like hell to me and I don't like them in my parlor. A smile doesn't cost anything but it could prove expensive not to smile. Unpainted faces and stringy hair is unattractive and being unattractive due to self negligence and laziness can prove costly.

"Boarders are expected to act like adults in the parlor at all times as well as in any other room here.

"The guests that come here are from all walks of life they are very much families with being treated as a guest should be treated. If any one here doesn't know how to treat a guest properly they haven't been educated in the right way as perhaps they need a refresher course else where no training are available here. I don't always agree with the old motto, the customer is always right, but I don't ignore it altogether either not anyone can please everyone in the world all the time but it sure would be nicer if everyone tried to always do right.

"Anytime a boarder has a friend in the parlor she is to sit with him until he is ready to leave or until she is busy with another friend. I don't want any man to be left alone in the parlor just so a boarder could to go to a hen session.

"Also when any boarder has a friend waiting on her the man is to be permitted to wait for her as long as he desires, if the man decides to change his mind it is to his own decision. I don't want another boarder trying to coax another boarders friend into not waiting for her. A boarder caught doing so will only be here long enough to get her things together and get out.

"Boarders are to go the doctor on Monday, Tuesday, or Wednesday before 11:30 a.m. or after 2:30 p.m. Boarders are to go to another doctor only when the regular doctor in on vaction or can't handle the case.

"All health cards are to put in the drawer in the check room. Any boarder without their health card kept up to date will not live here. Weekly smears are to be gotten at the doctor office and blood is to be gotten every ninety days.

"Any laxiety on the part of any boarder in adherring to the medical rules will result in immediate check out.

"When going to the doctor or shopping every boarder will wear a street dress of reasonable length. Not shorther than 2″ above the knee and a complete set of undergarments including hose, pants, and shorts are absolutely prohibited.

"Boarders are not permitted to go into any beer place in town or any cafe in town.

"Listed below is a list of permissables for boarders to go when in town. [Deleted]

"I could stay here writing forever but I consider the foregoing rules sufficient at this time, there are of course many other things to be considered and I expect a girl to ask me or whomever is in charge."

[11]

Marvin Zindler: Motives, Methods, and a Media Massacre

Marvin Zindler could have chosen to stay and run the family store in Houston, but somewhere during his formative years he was obviously brainwashed by too many movies featuring the good guys in the white hats. Substituting a blonde toupee, Marvin cast himself in the role of hero, completing his costume with well-tailored suits molded over pads on shoulders and buttocks. And the Zindler nose had to go! Both the nose and the chin fell under the knife and emerged with classic porportions.

After playing a few bit parts, Marvin managed to land his first big hero role as head of the Consumer Protection Division of the Harris County sheriff's office. Villainous car dealers, magazine salesmen, roofers, siders, and unfair advertisers all fell under his vengeful wrath. But they fell on Marvin's schedule. As director and superstar of his own production, Marvin was calling the shots and there would be no shots until a camera was ready to roll. He always made sure that all members of the news media could be in attendance whenever he was ready to do battle with the wicked entrepreneurs preying on widows and children.

He has been known to hold up for days on serving a warrant if a TV camera crew was not immediately available. In fact, this has been his modus operandi since first becoming a plain ole' deputy. Marvin also has served time as a police reporter for a Houston radio station, a job he was well-prepared for. He had been writing his own action-packed press releases years before going into broadcasting. The underprivileged consumer looked upon Marvin as a saviour, the news media looked upon him as a jerk, and the new sheriff in Harris County replaced him a couple of days after taking office.

When the Chicken Ranch heard its death toll Marvin was, officially, Consumer Affairs reporter for Houston's Channel 13, KTRK-TV. Unofficially, he was somewhat more, being their number one draw in the audience-survey ratings game and also the station's own best guest, filling in on any and all shows that needed a boost in ratings. As a self-acknowledged egomaniac Marvin was only too flattered to make public appearances. At one of the fund-raising affairs being emceed by various guest celebrities, the audience was asked to bid on donated merchandise. When Marvin Zindler took over the mike there were considerably more "boos" than "yeas," and the audience offered donations in various amounts for an assortment of physical abuse. For instance, a slap brought a bid for $5; a real punch for $10; and punching him way out brought an offer of $100. Marvin would not accept this generosity, however, and the audience was rather bitter about his poor sportsmanship. Fellow emcee Bill Mayne smoothed their ruffled feathers by forcibly removing Marvin's necktie and auctioning it to the highest bidder.

Marvin's chores on Channel 13 were similar to the tasks he carried out while still in the sheriff's office. Only the indictments were different. He had been serving warrants, but now the indictments came directly through TV, a method that is much more effective.

When accused of media-mongering, Marvin had a very rational reply. "Most corporations involved in, say, false advertising will just laugh at a fifty-dollar fine, but if you show up with a TV camera and give 'em bad publicity then they will shape up."

How did he get involved with a small-time country whorehouse a long way from home? Marvin quickly points out, "I'm no moralist," and makes it quite clear that he was not motivated by an indignant disgust at the moral laxity synonymous with whoring.

According to Marvin, he had no quarrel with the Chicken Ranch or any of the "carryings on" that the house was famous for. The dragons to be slain were those twin devils: political corruption and organized crime. Marvin claims to have seen a copy of an intelligence report compiled by the Department of Public Safety, and according to Marvin, the report claimed that the Chicken Ranch and another small cathouse down the road a few miles, in Sealy, Texas, to be exact, were grossing in excess of $3 million a year. The report supposedly stated that the majority of this money was going into Mexican bank accounts belonging to corrupt state and local officials who had received this fortune in the form of payoffs. And, says Marv, it's really those politicians who owned the Chicken Ranch, whose power at the state capital allowed them to stay open, and who promoted the continued success of the business.

The mention of organized crime usually brings to mind the Mafia, but Marvin uses the term loosely. Two eight-year-olds planning a cookie-jar heist could qualify. Although Marvin has always been vague about an exact description when using the term organized crime in reference to the Chicken Ranch, the only evidence of any type of organization is the grapevine from one cathouse to another that serves primarily as a job-referral source. Prostitutes do not walk into an employment agency seeking a position, the girls do not have a labor union to represent them, and they have no lobbyists in Washington. A loosely woven network of friends and acquaintances serves these purposes, and they do so with more loyalty and integrity than their counterparts in big business. It is "organized," but hardly constitutes "crime."

At any rate, these were the demons that Marvin wanted exorcized. He says he first saw the report in January 1973. At that time the Texas Rangers asked him not to do anything about it because they planned to "move in." In May Marvin got word through some grapevine of his own that the report and any action pertaining to it had been shelved. That did it! Marvin was mad. The whole thing just proved to him that somebody from higher up was interfering with enforcement of the law.

Marvin and a fellow newsman from KTRK-TV, Larry Connors, began an underground investigation. They spent long, hard hours sitting in the mosquito, chigger- and tick-infested woods outside the Chicken Ranch, counting cars and patrons and taking still photographs. Larry Connors volunteered courageously for "inside reconnaissance" and made the fantastic discovery that "there was whoring going on in there!"

Obviously, the two sleuths were enjoying their work; it took three months of this sort of "inside investigation" before they decided that they had ample evidence to prove that there was indeed a whorehouse in La Grange. Marvin had his trusty TV cameras brought to the scene and ran his exposé, informing the viewers in Houston of something every goat roper and cedar chopper in the state of Texas had been aware of since puberty.

Marvin's exposé was no one-shot deal. It was on every night with new developments and risqué revelations. There were interviews with Sheriff Jim that could be classified only as disastrous for the Sheriff. As an honest man he gave honest answers, something a real politician would never dream of doing.

After a week of these "further developments" Marvin went to Austin for an interview with Governor Dolph Briscoe himself on Monday, August 1, 1973. He also scheduled interviews with Attorney General John Hill and the Department of Public Safety Chief, Colonel Wilson Speir. The group met behind closed doors, and although Marvin's allegations about organized crime and political connections were never proven, The Big Three emerged from the meeting spouting righteous indignation and promises to get to the bottom of things.

Dolph said that he had read something or other about the Chicken Ranch in some paper several years earlier but the place had never been brought to his attention since. Colonel Speir said that his office had the house under surveillance for two months in an effort to link it with organized crime, but they had not been able to see any connection.

Attorney General John Hill told reporters after the "Big Three" meeting that there would be a meeting on the following Thursday with the three state officers and Sheriff T. J. Flournoy. "We all feel the laws of the State cannot be selectively enforced," said Hill. "You've got a situation where the law is not being enforced on a local level. We're going to say to the local people, 'We want the law enforced and we want it enforced now.' "

The Sheriff received his summons to appear before the governor on Thursday and he realized that time had run out. If he did not have the house closed down, the Texas Rangers would.

His big hand rested loosely on the phone, postponing for another minute, then two. "I'm not too old to believe in miracles," he told himself. "Dolph Briscoe may be governor, but he ain't God."

The sheriff slouched in his old swivel chair, recalling those times when one of his favorite dogs or horses had to be destroyed—he always did the job himself. It would have been easier to let a stranger do it, but in their final defeat and agony loved ones should not have to deal with strangers. It is a private moment to share their loss and sorrow.

That is how he felt now. He experienced an odd mixture of sadness and embarrassment, deep sorrow and sympathy for a good friend who was being hurt, and anger and bitterness because he was the instrument who had to deliver the hurt. But there was no alternative. The Chicken Ranch would be closed, if not by him, then by the Texas Rangers or some other branch of the law. His way would be quick with no sensationalism for the vultures of the news media to feed on. Perhaps he and Edna could both salvage some measure of dignity after this totally unnecessary fiasco was over. Those damned reporters were sure going to be disappointed!

The sheriff tried, but he could not find any reasonable excuse for having to put Edna and her girls out of work. If the citizens who had elected him had found it necessary to close the ranch for some reason, he would have accepted their decision and respected their wishes. If Edna and her personnel were jeopardizing the health, wealth, or the moral scruples of the people who had elected him to enforce the laws, or, if the place had even been just a nasty nuisance, an eyesore, or even a fire hazard—just something that would justify his actions—he would have tried his best to understand another point of view. But there was no reason.

There had been no reason for Marvin Zindler to do his muckraking so far from his own stompin' grounds. Houston had one hundred times the number of prostitutes in Fayette County. It the Houston television audience loved Marvin so much, they would have endorsed him enthusiastically in his efforts to clean up their own town—in theory at least.

But Marvin was not seeking salvation through good deeds; Marvin was seeking publicity through any deeds, whether good, rotten, or indifferent. Busting sixteen obscure whores from Houston was not going to grab any headlines. But the Chicken Ranch was not obscure; it was a name familiar to every schoolboy in Texas. The house was doomed for destruction because its public relations had worked too well.

[12]

Showdown: Victims, Villains, and Vindication

LA GRANGE, Tex. (AP)—Bitter and grim-voiced, Sheriff T. J. Flournoy reacted to gubernatorial pressure Wednesday and closed Texas' oldest bawdy house.

"It's been there all my life and all my daddy's life and never caused anybody any trouble," Flournoy said. "Every large city in Texas has things 1,000 times worse." [*Austin American-Statesman* August 2, 1973]

The sheriff had done his duty as both lawman and friend—and he felt like hell. By Tuesday night the girls were packing their clothes, the doorbell went unanswered. A phone call was answered by a maid. She was asked if the house was closed, and answered, "I just can't tell you, honey. I just don't know anything about that."

By Wednesday morning the girls were gone from La Grange, and Marvin was on his way to Jamaica on vacation. The only person remaining at the Ranch was Lilly, the maid, shooing off the curious and accepting sympathy and condolences from old friends and customers.

The sheriff had managed to collect several thousand signatures on a petition to the governor asking that the house be allowed to remain open. He had kept his Thursday appointment in Austin, and took the lengthy petition with him. But the Governor's office had cancelled the meeting after announcing to newsmen that the house had been closed permanently. "That settles the matter," said the chief executive, as he left to give a speech on "Cargo Security," leaving Big Jim holding his hat and his petition.

Housewives, teachers, and dowagers were included in the names on the petition. The editor of the *La Grange Journal*, Lester Zapalac, took an editorial stand on the issue.

"I think it's alright. There's no organized crime attached to it, and its beneficial to the community," he said. "I've never seen anything bad come from it and I've lived here all my life. The girls buy all their clothes here, their eats. It brings in business for the community."

"They pay taxes same as everybody else"; continues the editor, "It keeps down rape, venereal disease. I think most of the people here are in favor of it."

When county employee, Albert Huebel, was asked if he thought it a good or bad idea to close the house, he replied, "I don't think it was a good idea. You take a lot of young boys, they're going to be looking for women. If they can't find 'em, they'll rape 'em, and if they don't do that they'll run to other women and get diseases. These girls went to doctors.

"The men that didn't want to go there, they didn't have to go there," he added.

The reasons for wanting it to remain open covered all bases, most of a general nature and some personal. One middle-aged housewife stated her interest in the continuation of the business quite emphatically, "Hell, it kept my old man from bothering me! If I wasn't in the mood I'd just as soon have him go on up the road."

But it was the girls from the Ranch who took to the road—to Houston, Dallas, and Austin, with Austin absorbing the majority. Austin's massage parlors made good use of their multiple talents until Travis County elected a new sheriff who in turn elected to close the massage parlors (temporarily). He has since established an abysmal track record in solving murders, and Austin has more prostitution then ever, plus heroin addicts in record number. The Chicken Ranch whores left Austin for Houston, where Marvin Zindler would not notice them.

Edna got married after her forced retirement and moved to a small East Texas town where her husband owns a couple of restaurants. But she did not go directly there. Her first move was to purchase a nice retirement home in La Grange, among the people who had always liked her so well. She selected a comfortable house in the nicest part of town, in the neighborhood where Sheriff Jim lived with his wife, Gladys. But her down payment was returned. These nice folks, who had liked her, befriended her, and supported her livelihood for so long, did not want her *living* in their town.

Customers for the ranch continued to show up in La Grange more than two years after the house had been closed. Many a local girl capitalized on their disappointment—sometimes to the tune of 200 dollars. There were also a few local amateurs taking in "callers," and the sheriff knew exactly who and where they were.

On December 30, 1974, one year after the Chicken Ranch was closed, Marvin came back to town to do a documentary on the economic impact the closing had on the town. He and a camera man interviewed several people and their final interview for the afternoon was with the sheriff.

Needless to say, the sheriff had no love for Marvin. He made a point of telling him so, expletives included, and when Marvin had the audacity to speak up, the sheriff shoved him, took his camera, and ripped out the film. To add insult to injury, Marvin's wig fell off and Big Jim stomped it with his cowboy boots. But according to Marvin's three million dollar lawsuit, the Sheriff not only busted his camera, he fractured some of Marvin's ribs as well.

The local folk came to the defense of their hero. By June, 1975 they held a barbecue and sold bumper stickers to raise funds for the suit against Flournoy and Fayette County. Jim's first lawyer was Richard (Racehorse) Haynes, but he had to retain a different one because Haynes was busy with the defense of O. P. Carillo, another politico caught with his hand in the cookie jar. (Haynes's reputation as a shrewd defense lawyer spread nationwide in 1977 when he successfully defended Fort Worth multimillionaire Cullen Davis, charged with murdering his stepdaughter.)

When Sheriff Flournoy was asked why he had not hired the famous Houston attorney, Percy Foreman, he said, "I'd never use that man, because I've seen Foreman get too many people off who should have rightfully gone to jail."

In September the sheriff asked that all soliciting of funds cease. He wanted no more publicity. He even asked the local stores to stop selling Chicken Ranch T-shirts and other souvenirs. They were taken off display, but they could still be purchased under-the-counter. Local consensus at that time was that the trial would never come to pass; it would be postponed because of Jim's bad health, and Jim would eventually die before standing trial. Defense monies raised were only a pittance compared to $3 million.

Local consensus was correct. There never was a trial, but not because of Jim's bad health or postponements. It was settled out-of-court, and the amount was never revealed. Rumor says Marvin got $10,000.

There is still a great deal of interest in the Chicken Ranch. A disc jockey from Houston asked Jim's brother, Sheriff Mike Flournoy, to get him a bed from the Ranch so that he could auction it off at a fund raiser. The disc jockey said he could probably get $5000 for it, but Mike could not, or would not, deliver the bed.

It was reported that some lawyers from Houston had purchased the house and were planning to make a restaurant out of it, the bedrooms serving as individual dining rooms. The owner of the Cottonwood Restaurant (*everyone's* favorite stop between Houston and Austin) said that he wished that Edna had offered it to him before selling to the lawyers, as he would have liked to buy it.

Rumors were rampant and Edna was reported in several locations after the Chicken Ranch closed. She was reported to be in Austin with her sister, Hattie Valdez (Hattie had no sister), in Nevada, where prostitution is legal, in Houston running a house, and in Florida where she had vast real estate holdings. None of these reports were true. According to a man in La Grange who claims to be her best friend, Edna moved to Gladewater, Texas, with her husband, Glenn Davidson. He also said, "She has very little money."

It was rumored that some of the girls from the Chicken Ranch were in Midland, Texas, running a house out of a trailer park. A check revealed that no one there had heard of it; however, there was a cocktail lounge there called the Chicken Ranch that was popular with hookers, and some may have worked at the original.

In 1977 the building that has housed the most enduring business in La Grange was moved to Dallas, Texas, and reopened as a bar/discotheque/restaurant specializing in chicken dishes. It was deliberately left in its original, somewhat shabby condition. Anyone who had scratched his name on the wall during a previous visit would still be able to find it there. Edna Milton was the hostess! But this business was not successful. Plagued by heating problems and a lack of customers, the restaurant closed.

Sheriff T. J. (Jim) Flournoy ran for re-election in May 1976. His only opponent (the second one he had ever had during his political career) was a mechanic. Jim never really considered him a *serious* opponent. He wasn't—Jim won by a landslide.

Jim was 79 years old in 1979, and still Sheriff of Fayette County.

CPSIA information can be obtained
at www.ICGtesting.com
Printed in the USA
BVHW081432151219
566734BV00002B/237/P

9 780595 128488